Villains, Victims & the Vanquished: A Memoir

Joseph Morin

Published by Joseph Morin, 2021.

While every precaution has been taken in the preparation of this book, the publisher assumes no responsibility for errors or omissions, or for damages resulting from the use of the information contained herein.

VILLAINS, VICTIMS & THE VANQUISHED: A MEMOIR

First edition. October 15, 2021.

Copyright © 2021 Joseph Morin.

ISBN: 979-8201809317

Written by Joseph Morin.

Table of Contents

To my dear wife Carol, for her many years of loving support. My journey would have been half empty without her. Her steadfast belief in me kept my shoulder to the wheel, especially when the terrain got bumpy. It couldn't have been easy for her but she made it seem so.

To the many children who taught me along the way. Their paths were never straight but they endured the best way they knew how.

Finally, to my friends and family who may have wondered what I did with my days at school and why I did it. This is so you will know.

The recounting of a life is a cheat, of course: I admit the truth of this; even our own stories are obscenely distorted; it is a wonder really that we keep faith with the simple container of our existence.

Carol Shields, The Stone Diaries

Chapter 1: Introduction

This memoir encompasses my four-decade-long journey working with students who have unique disabilities. Over the years, my experiences with these students extended from my role as both a General Education Teacher and as a Special Education Teacher. In these roles, I worked at all three levels of community schooling: elementary, middle, and high school. In addition, I taught in a few specialized residential settings. During the final phase of my career, I was a Professor of Special Education at the University of Wisconsin – Eau Claire. There, I instructed student teachers and guided other professionals-in-training in clinical settings. I did this until my retirement in 2014. The entire span of my career in education was 44 years.

Why a memoir? This is a fair question, one I'm not sure I can supply a complete answer to. At the tail-end of my career, I was teaching a course on academic assessment to undergraduates. The course was compulsory, technically specific, and a minimum standard of B+ was required. It was a bit of a slog for them, as the course may not have aligned well with their assumed role. I was okay with the challenge of combatting these attitudinal headwinds but became a bit weary of it all toward the end. I began to question my relevance. It was an odd feeling and one I couldn't seem to shake. It may have been the immaturity of my students. It may have been my sense that there was a tectonic drift in modern education toward what I perceived to be nebulous directions. It may even have been my age—I was approaching 65. Whatever it was, I couldn't rid myself of the feeling. It was time to go. But now, some six years later, I am lamenting. I feel I may have left something behind. So, I suppose this memoir is to reach back, collect some thoughts, consolidate some of the more influential experiences I had along the way, and reflect on them from the sturdy perch of my accumulated wisdom—following the breadcrumbs as it were. I believe this exercise will be beneficial for young teachers just starting out, as it may provide them with a beacon of light—not to show them the way, but to let them know there is a path that has been travelled before. This memoir might also benefit those non-teachers who have an inclination for critically examining the broader social construct of schooling as it serves (or in some cases underserves) children, especially children with disabilities. Other readers might simply enjoy being introduced to the astonishing variety of students that comprise the spectrum of disability encountered in a Special Education classroom.

But let's be honest. My motive for this memoir isn't practical, and if any pedagogical benefit is derived from it's reading, it will be entirely accidental. So, I suppose my true motive is so others will know. And, by others, I mean the many non-educators who have, in my presence, expressed over-simplified opinions on schools and schooling. They may have claimed to know what a "good" or "bad" school looks like—whether a teacher is competent or not, or whether the curriculum is appropriate. Often, these opinions have been wrought from their own apprenticeships of once having been a student. I believe this endows them with a false sense of entitlement. *It's not the way I learned* you may hear. In my view, this perspective clogs the mind. Sometimes these individuals are my friends or family, and their dismissal of the possibility that I may have a more informed perspective has left me annoyed, even hurt. Regretfully, I have abandoned attempts to convince them otherwise. I have found such conversations can become uncomfortable and, unfortunately, unconvincing. I am hoping the uniqueness of the case studies I have introduced will immerse them into the complexity of the Special Educator's task and thus, encourage a greater appreciation of the work. For this, I would be grateful.

And now the title, *Villains, Victims, and the Vanquished*, the "3-Vs". The 3-Vs form the perceptual foundation for my practice as a Special Educator. The terms do not sound particularly positive, do they? Disparaging even. I do not want this to be misconstrued, so I will deal with it right up front. Special Educators serve students with disabilities, be they physical, cognitive, or emotional. This group of educators see anomalous development in full view every single day. Each will process what they experience through their own unique lens. These perceptions, conscious or otherwise, influence their interactions with students in significant ways. It is my view that whether these interactions are beneficial or less so, perhaps even harmful, largely depends on the lens they peer through. Consider a disruptive child, for example, upsetting a desk or spewing invective at a teacher or a classmate. If viewed as a *villain*, the teacher might disregard the possibility that the child has experienced enormous strife in their life and imprudently exert a punitive strategy that is not only excessive, but quite possibly results in exacerbating the child's difficulties. Another example: a child with Down syndrome might get more assistance on a task than needed. This may inadvertently hamper the child's development (e.g., by contributing to a learned helplessness) as they are protected from the "pain" of experiencing more frustration. At the heart of the overly helpful response might be the perception of the child as a *victim* of their genetic condition (i.e., the genetic anomaly of an extra chromosome). The sympathetic judgement (i.e., feeling sorry for the child), although not intentionally harmful, may inadvertently discourage greater independence—an unwanted outcome for a child whose primary goal should be as much independence as is appropriate. Finally, the insidiousness of the perception of *vanquishment* for those children who struggle with learning—holding low expectations for them. This perception has been known to hobble educators' view of these children's academic horizons. The damage this view holds has been observed for over half a century (i.e., the Pygmalion or Rosenthal effect[1]). In these ways, the 3-Vs swirl around, surreptitiously nudging the educator's actions and reactions in ways that are not always beneficial. In the episodes that follow, the 3-Vs will be thrumming in the background, and the reader will be embroiled in a perception-forming vortex whether they are aware of it or not. The choice of one lens or the other may not appear as a choice at all—something that just seeps in, only noticed after deep contemplation and often, too late.

A cautionary note: I will be introducing episodes with students who I have found to be extraordinarily interesting. The anecdotes accrue from my extensive experiences with students with disabilities. I hope readers are as drawn to these students' stories as I was; however, I must confess to grappling with an ethical issue. I am fearful that my account of these children's lives will unintentionally brand them as *curiosities* and nothing more. This would be a crime; one I do not wish to perpetrate. I cannot deny that the children remembered here have been selected for their uniqueness, and in the telling of their story, I may have pushed to the fore uncomplimentary images, even disparaging ones; for this, I ask the reader's indulgence. It is not my intention to strip these children of their dignity. They functioned within a context of disadvantage, and it is my view they could only do what they were able to do at the time. I will further caution that these accounts will likely lead the reader into the world of the abnormal. No doubt, judgements will be rendered. I cannot defend against this rendering other than to steer readers toward the possibility that these children were formed from an alchemy of less-than-ideal influences that impeded their development in various ways: functionally, socially, psychologically, and academically. The following pages include a dozen or so accounts, but readers should note that there are hundreds of other children not included in this memoir. I'll confess to an arbitrary process here, isolating only the most unusual memories, but I would like readers to know that the majority of interactions Special Educators have with students with disabilities are not nearly as unusual as the ones presented here.

I must also alert readers to the family-context where these children's lives were fostered. Some families may appear startlingly dysfunctional. This is the danger I have inherited in my task. When one begins to extricate an anecdote from a historical context, it is usually at the risk of lopping off a piece of complexity which may be fundamental to arriving at a fuller understanding of the child. I fear my ability to do justice to these children's complex lives will be insufficient and negative judgements may proliferate. I will make my view clear here. Parents and other caretakers have been navigating their own journeys and conquering their own demons. Where they sit on the spectrum of virtue is not for me to decide. Where transgressions seem obvious, I do not forgive them, but rather acknowledge the challenges that confronted them at the time and feel deep empathy for their circumstances. When instructing in my university classes, I would often warn student teachers and school psychologists-in-training about the dangers of forming judgements placed on students' families. I would remind them that these children are returning to homes that we do not reside in. More importantly, we will be absent from these children's lives long after they leave our classrooms or, our assessment centres. These families may not be able to remove themselves from the reality they live in, and whatever decision made on their child's behalf, be it good or bad, the only ones in the room that must live with these decisions are the family members. I am hoping readers will recognize this as they are introduced to the accounts I will be sharing.

Forgive me for stating the obvious, but I wanted to ensure readers that I have thought this through. This is a memoir and, as such, is unavoidably subjective. I am priming the pump of my own memory, and in doing so, I am aware that the light falls where I position my gaze. In the shadows, there may be memories I have overlooked or perhaps hidden away. Through this preferential sifting, I may have unintentionally embellished my contribution or inflated my attributes, boasting if you will. True, I am proud of my career and feel that in most cases students were well served by me. But in honesty, through the success I may have enjoyed along the way, I have also erred, and even ashamed of what I did or did not do in a few situations. I would hope though, on balance, I have done a good job, and if I could meet these students again, they would say (hopefully, with a knowing smile), "I remember you; you were my teacher," For that I would be thankful.

Finally, please note that I have protected the identities of all the children introduced in this memoir by giving them fictitious names.

Chapter 2: George, Brian, and Me

I was in my third year of teaching when things began to shift for me. It was a matter of perspective that changed the most. I was recruited to work in an outdoor school after spending my first two years as a 4th grade teacher in a suburban elementary school. This outdoor school (I'll refer to it as SJ) was situated in a rural community just outside of a large metropolitan area. SJ served students in the 6th grade, providing aspects of typical curriculum but using activities in the out-of-doors as the textbook. Students stayed for a full week, sleeping in dormitories, and eating in a cafeteria. A central classroom was used to consolidate their outdoor experiences. Topics such as orienteering, edible wild foods, mapping, ornithology, geology, geography, survival skills, and a smattering of season-specific activities such as cross-country skiing and snowshoeing were offered. Periodically, our staff would arrange visits to local potters, glass-blowers, and weavers. Some visiting classes would learn agriculture using a working farm that was in the area. There was even a wealthy gentleman-farmer whose hobby was sheep husbandry, and he took great delight in demonstrating how he and his dog herded them. I must confess that this was my favourite activity and, judging from the wide-eyed response from the students, it was theirs as well. When the week was over, the students would return to their home communities, bubbling with an irrepressible excitement for learning. It may have even endured beyond the first week back, but that might be a bit of a reach given their ages. Regardless, it was a wonderful experience for the students, one which I would have enjoyed as a youngster myself.

I am meandering a bit. Let me get back to the title of the chapter: George, Brian, and Me. At SJ, one week of the entire academic year was dedicated to a group of students with social and emotional needs. During this week, students from around the region were selected from what were then called "Sensitivity Classes" situated in schools from around the region. These students were identified by school personnel who felt the students' needs were significant enough to warrant a special approach. They were classified as children with emotional disabilities (ED) and their lack of emotional regulation was such that their schooling occurred in segregated settings. Along with these students—there were about 25 of them—was a cluster of behavioural specialists (i.e., social workers, youth-care specialists, school psychologists) who coordinated the one-week program. Naturally, the week focused on behavioural health facilitated in a novel educational setting, the out-of-doors. The curriculum wasn't much different than it was for other groups that spent time at SJ, but the addition of the trained professionals to help the children work through their social and emotional difficulties was unique. Up to that point in my career, I had no experience with this population, and to be frank, I wasn't looking forward to it. The week was something that I had to endure and the sooner it was over the better. That was my perspective. Little did I know that it would be this week that would change the trajectory of my entire teaching career.

Now for George. George was the custodian at SJ. He was hired hastily, as our expected custodian had a change of heart just before the school year was to begin. With this sudden vacancy, Wilf (our principal) was in a jam and hired George on the spot even though he had some reservations about how he presented. George was a gruff sort in his 50s. He was tall and lean and had an angular face, frozen in a perpetual grimace, his eyes conveying a dark, brooding soul. Wilf provided him with a custodian's shirt with GEORGE written on it, but after the first week I never saw that shirt again. He was that kind of guy. Of the scant personal details shared with me over the few months he worked at SJ, I learned he was divorced and had a couple of adult sons who were estranged from him. He had a small horse farm that specialized in Appaloosa horses. It was only a few concession roads over from SJ, so it was close by and handy for him to tend to his farm chores before and after work, as well as during the odd lunch break. George wasn't a career custodian. He took the job reluctantly, as he had been abruptly laid-off from his lineman job of twenty years at the hydro company. To say that he was grumpy about this would be an understatement. This grumpiness affected his work, as he only did what he had to do. Nothing more. George usually kept to himself most of the time, unless, in his eye at least, something was amiss; then, you knew about it. It could be where a car was parked in error, a coat improperly hung, or a piece of equipment that was poorly stored. If kids traipsed through a newly mopped floor with dirty feet, his objection to their lack of considerateness boiled over and they felt the hot breath of his wrath. The subtlety of a positive behavioural approach escaped him. He probably despised it as *touchy-feely hogwash*. A harsh rebuff was his preferred choice to deal with "misbehaviour". Clearly, most kids irritated him, so I was particularly on edge when the kids with ED showed up for their week-long therapy session in the out-of-doors. I feared there might be an incident that I would have to mediate. It turns out I was wrong, very wrong. I discovered this when I found George eating his lunch with Brian.

Brian, one of the students with ED, had endured enough trauma in his short life to render even the most emotionally resilient child, unsalvageable. Readers should know that I am recalling information from forty years back, so what I knew of Brian back then was far more than what I am recalling now. I remember Brian's head being misshaped, a bit lopsided in one of his temples. There was a nasty scar on the protrusion. It was an ominous reminder of the surgery that was required to relieve the swelling in his brain, the result of a non-accidental blow to the head. That, and a trail of withered flesh leading down his neck on to his shoulder told volumes about Brian's background. The scalding was from a boiling pot of soup that was thrown at him by an enraged parent. It was no surprise he was an angry kid, and it was also no surprise that he displaced this anger often and indiscriminately, without much concern for the consequences.

As I recall, Brian's behaviour wasn't much different than the other kids' that had attended that week. Resistance, non-compliance, swearing, and aggression toward others (including staff) could be expected from any one of the students, and Brian was no exception. So, seeing George sitting alone with this troubled young boy was a shocker; eating hot dogs and seemingly enjoying each other's company. But that was only the beginning of the shock for me.

The week was an exhausting one and getting the youngsters packed up and on to the bus signalled an enormous relief. I had survived! And apparently, George did as well. He even hung around to say goodbye, and that was a first. He never did that. His job was to mop up after the last student boarded the bus, but he'd usually get a head start by attacking vacant parts of the building while the students were assembling in the lobby. This time was different though. He was actually helping students get their bags on to the bus. He even kibitzed with a few, especially Brian. It was good to see but strangely out of character. After the students were all accounted for, I gave the bus driver the nod and they headed down the road. I turned abruptly and caught George waiving vigorously. At that moment we locked eyes. Nothing was said to elicit conversation, but George began talking about Brian. It wasn't much, a bit stammered when, in mid-sentence, he teared up. He couldn't finish what he was going to say. The moment was awkward and it didn't last long. He eventually turned and returned to his chores, his thoughts unfinished.

I don't know how or when George's connection with Brian was spawned. He may have overheard some of the staff talking about Brian's background while he was sweeping the hall. He may have peeked at a confidential dossier of the group left on top of the filing cabinet in the office when he was emptying the trash. Or, he may have just been drawn in by Brian's overt neediness. I don't really know. Here's the point though. His perception changed, and changed dramatically. It changed how he chose to respond to behaviours he formerly found objectionable to the point where a budding relationship was kindled. Clearly, something happened and Brian became someone other than just another intolerable youth. George must have seen Brian's *victimhood*—a victim of reprehensible circumstances. Empathy became his guide much like an emergency-room nurse doesn't scold the accident victim for screaming as their wounds are being tended to. Brian, much like the patient, must have been perceived to have had no volitional control over his behaviour, and that switch in George's perception wedged the door open for a positive interaction.

George never became Brian's "Big Brother". Nothing like that. He never saw Brian again as far as I know. (George left after Christmas.) However, that last day of that exhausting week and that ever-so-tender moment in the parking lot as we waived goodbye to the bus, a bus filled with kids just like Brian, formed the foundation for how I came to understand dysfunctional behaviour—behaviour that is often acquired in response to circumstances found in the darkest corners of young person's development. They weren't just "bad kids". Of course, it wasn't my observation of the two of them bonding that did it. It was more than that. During that week, I witnessed some deceptively simple but astonishingly effective techniques of de-escalation and treatment that I had never seen before. I saw pro-social behaviours being taught, not just expected. I learned, just as reading and arithmetic must be taught so must pro-social behaviour, and there are non-punitive ways of teaching it that are far more enduring than through tough discipline. I saw these things, but by no means could I do any of them. I knew I had to learn more. I was intrigued, intrigued enough to certify as a Special Educator.

Chapter 3: Reality

I took the steps to become certified to teach Special Education. This involved taking courses that would lead me in that direction. You would think that this path of enlightenment would make me feel more prepared for my new role. I was wrong. After completing the half-dozen or so extra certification courses, I was barely more competent than I was when I began. But I didn't know it. Not until I stepped into my first Special Education classroom that is.

I was in year five of my career when my new certification was completed, and I accepted a Special Education position in a small town of about ten thousand people, an hour northwest of Toronto. As I recall, there were about ten children assigned to my classroom that year, about the average number of children for this type of classroom. I'll highlight some of these students to provide the reader with a brief understanding of the diverse nature of the group I had acquired.

Gerald was about ten. He had cognitive disabilities (referred to as mental retardation back then) that put him about three years behind academically. His social maturity was well below that. He would tantrum like a two-year-old if he didn't get his way. He would resort to baby-talk if he wanted attention. Michael was his foster brother. Michael was about the same age as Gerald but much more advanced academically. He could read and comprehend material well past his grade level. His ability with mathematics was not on the same level, but it was more than adequate. His needs for special programming arose from his psychological challenges. At the time, the school psychologist suspected Michael might be demonstrating signs of childhood schizophrenia, an earlier term for autism. He had a far-away look in his eye and there was a mystic quality to his voice as he spoke, as if he were in a dream state. He had troublesome obsessions that interfered with the goals of his schooling. For example, he was obsessed with holes in structures. They were mysterious to him and he probed them endlessly, sticking things in them. It might be a tiny pinhole in the mortar between the bricks on a wall or the large drainage grate over the stormwater pipe. He would displace enormous energy detecting holes wherever he was situated—the classroom, the hallway, the school yard. It was not only a distraction but also potentially dangerous. One day he gave the whole school a day off. He had plugged a drainage culvert in the school yard with sticks. The dam that formed prevented water from escaping, and an overnight deluge backed up water into the building, rendering it unusable for that day. The other children may have been thrilled, but the principal and the parents were anything but pleased. Another student, Roger was about nine and was adopted by a family who ran a religious commune. He was a year or two behind his age academically. He had been badly abused by his biological parents and suffered from enormous anxiety because of it. You had to be very cognizant of that when you were correcting him. The most benign reprimand or academic redirection would elicit a dramatic melt-down. The category of attention-deficit – hyperactivity disorder (ADHD) had not yet emerged in the literature at that time, but I am reasonably certain he would have been a prime candidate. He was constantly fidgeting, and his attention to instruction could be measured in seconds rather than minutes. Tracy was a cute little girl of five or six. She was autistic, severely so. She had no receptive or expressive language that you could build on. She would scream and cry for no apparent reason and would laugh uncontrollably without anything remotely humorous happening. I can recall her always holding a small length of yarn in her fingers. She could play with that for hours on end, and attempts to replace it with something more appropriate would result in uncontrollable bouts of screaming. This scraggly piece of yarn was her preferred toy, while toys more typical of her age and gender went untouched. There were a few other children as well. Their needs would have been more toward academic remediation necessitating a re-design of instructional materials and modifications to the pacing of lessons. The point is, the constant need to juggle the variables that beset me was exhausting.

So, this unique group of individuals comprised my new reality, and as mentioned, I knew from the moment I walked into that classroom that my training, such as it was, was woefully inadequate. Here I was, a "specialist" but in name only. I felt terribly incompetent. I may have known more than I thought, but I couldn't recognize it at the time. I had one solid asset and that was my willingness to figure it out. I needed time, and I wasn't sure those I was accountable to (e.g., parents, the principal) would be all that forgiving if things didn't go well.

I want to clarify something about my training though. Retrospectively, after over four decades of maturing into the field of Special Education—through extra certifications, a few graduate degrees, and boatloads of experiences—I can not conceive of any course work that would have better prepared me for that first year. So, I don't blame my certifying body. For now, it is enough to know that it was the best it could have been.

Some of the diversity of the group emerged from an equally diverse home life for the students in my Special Education class. Gerald and Michael lived in a group home for children in need of care. The matron (my word) of the home ran a militaristic type of family atmosphere. There were rules and punishments that would make most men and women in uniform twitch. If either of them forgot their lunch, they went without lunch the next day. If their clothes got stained, they would have to scrub them clean as soon as they returned from school. If it happened again, she would send them to school with instructions that a raincoat was to be worn throughout the day. These were a few of the things I remember, but there were many more. There was considerable consternation regarding the difference of opinion in what was best for Michael and Gerald. Once they left the building, they experienced the exact opposite of what I felt (and also what others felt) they truly needed—a nurturing environment that allowed for appropriate development. True, they were both housed, fed, and clothed but not much more.

As mentioned above, Roger was adopted. His family was a large one, consisting of other adopted children. It had a cult-like religious quality to it. His adopted parents expected him to pray a lot. If he got six out of ten on a math paper, he would need to dedicate a number of prayers for his mistakes. He was not allowed to play with neighbourhood children, as their boisterousness and foul language were thought to contaminate him. If there was something I suggested he work on at home, it would only get done if it didn't interfere with prayer time. None of this helped his anxiety level nor his progress in school. I suspect, Roger may have learned that the reason for his lack of academic achievement was "sinfulness". I may be overstating this, but the larger point is that while addressing Roger's academic and social needs, I also had to work within the context and limitations of his home life. It was not my place to interfere with his spiritual journey. He was not being abused. He was being cared for, and it just so happened, in the eyes of his adoptive parents at least, his spiritual needs took precedence over his academic and social ones. Parents know what is best for their children. Or do they?

I'll end with Tracy's family situation. She was the young girl with autism. Tracy's needs were extreme. She had come from a residential centre where she spent most of her early childhood. Among other things, this centre provided intense speech and language therapy as well as behavioural management. Still, with all this treatment, other than the odd word in sign language (e.g., bathroom, drink, food), her interactive language was non-existent. This must have been devastating for her young parents who desperately wanted their daughter home and attending a community school. When she finally became enrolled in our school, her parents found their very needy daughter had a young teacher who didn't have a clue what to do with her. That, of course, was me. While in my class, there were follow-up visits by the Speech and Language Pathologist who had worked with Tracy in the treatment centre where her initial education began. She would visit every couple of weeks and provide me with a few suggestions, but none of these suggestions incorporated the classroom context I was working in. They involved one-on-one activities that were so basic that they weren't in any way appropriate for the others, and I'm not even sure for her. I knew she needed more, but I didn't know what *more* was nor how to give it to her while also meeting the needs of the others. I knew it. The parents knew it. Everyone knew it. I felt terrible. If she was going to benefit from anything in my classroom, it would be through osmosis. That was my feeling at the time, and it is not a good feeling to have. Hope is not a useful strategy.

As with any teaching situation, progress-reporting is essential. We had to do it three times a year. I remember facing those first reports with dread. I knew I had done a lot with the students, and I was certain what I had done with them wasn't harmful, but I was less sure about the instructional benefit it provided. I may have been getting them to do some things that they already knew how to do. Or, I may have been trying to get them to do things that were way beyond their developmental readiness. I may even have been trying to get them to learn things that they really didn't need to know, things that were unnecessary for the trajectory of their complicated lives. For example, I can recall trying to teach Tracy the sounds letters make so that she could learn to decode written words. How relevant was this to language-less little girl? I was in a quandary.

With time things got better, and I was able to put the instruction I provided on a more secure footing. I was able to develop some routines and find curricular materials appropriate to the students' needs. The elusive goal of procuring evidence of growth gradually became more tangible. However, attributing all this growth to the instruction I provided may have been a bit presumptuous. I have since learned that there is a kind of melding that takes place when students (and parents) "get used" to you by glomming on to your approach, your routines, and your expectations—a sense of security settles in, and the day acquires more predictability to it. They know you better and, you them. In this way, a period of natural maturation takes place—growth occurring on its own due to forces outside of one's direct influence. However, there were a few very important lessons emerging in my development. I'll describe them here.

Firstly, effort can go a long way, even if it's misguided or bereft of obvious benefit. People seem to appreciate effort. *He must be doing a good job, look at him work!* one might think. I even convinced myself of this, perhaps hoping that extra effort might reveal the best path forward. Another realization I recognized is that very few people will trade you places in your role as a Special Educator, especially pedagogically messy ones like the one I had. They don't want (or maybe are unable) to do what you are attempting to do. That doesn't necessarily mean they don't value what you are doing, just that they know it's not for them. Lastly, the bar for success is usually low for Special Educators. People are not expecting you to produce Rhode Scholars. Their primary expectation is that you attempt to shape a hard-to-serve population of students and somehow transform them into a group that is less difficult to work with. As I say, it's a low bar and one that can easily give rise to complacency, if you let it.

All this leaves one with tremendous autonomy and a license to rely on self-judgement as your sole source of guidance. This can be both a positive and a negative. Being your own boss can be motivating or an exercise in self-deception. One has to be cautious. My first Special Education teaching assignment taught me this. Readers will recall Michael, mentioned above, could read and comprehend at a grade-level well beyond what his age would predict. I could take no credit for this strength, yet when visitors to my classroom observed Michael completing assignments from a 9th grade text, they were impressed by him and, indirectly, impressed by my apparent instruction. I had no agency over Michael's competence. The custodian could have provided him with the same task and the result would have been just as impressive. Michael had some innate abilities that were acquired independently of my intervention. When accolades are in short supply, it is tempting to claim successes that are not rightfully yours. This false sense of worthiness leaves you with an odd feeling when you are convinced that your performance is barely more than adequate.

A final lesson from this first year was my recognition of the importance of relationship-building and getting children to trust in you as a teacher and as a person. Trust is difficult to arrange for. It is wonderful when you have it and it's horrible when you don't. It might manifest itself in a level of compliance, a sharing of something fun, or a sharing of something that was troubling them. You can't demand it. You have to nurture it through the thick and thin of it all. They will have good days and bad days, as will you. One must respect their capacity to learn at any given moment and going from there was a big lesson for me.

This introduction to my chosen field was a brutal reality but one that filled me with mystery. The children were so immensely complicated, and I knew I wanted to be better than I was. I needed time and opportunities to do just that.

Chapter 4: Patience and Other Things

You must have a lot of patience. I cannot tell you how many times that particular statement was directed toward me when people found out I was a Special Education Teacher. I knew their comments were well-meaning, but it bothered me when I heard it. It took me a few years to articulate why exactly, but as I matured into my profession, I found myself challenging assumptions about this notion of "patience". I saw patience as something like height or eye-colour, nothing I had any agency over. Imagine a 10-foot basketball player dominating the NBA, scoring baskets at will by merely standing near the basket. I wonder how such a player would perceive his skill if his height were his only attribute? He wouldn't have to hone any of the other skills that make players "great". Patience is like that. It is a characteristic requiring no particular skill. It's passive, and if anything good comes from it, it is merely by chance. I was convinced *effectiveness* in my chosen field was much more than *patience*, and I was annoyed when I heard that galling phrase directed toward me and my practice.

Many of the competencies required in teaching are shared by mothers, fathers, and older siblings—anyone who teaches things that children learn as they develop. In this way, unlike other professions, teaching is a natural human (and non-human) activity and is essential for survival. Non-teachers often feel an innate kinship with formal teaching, as they themselves have served apprenticeships in school as students, often for a significant portion of their lives. They also have done some learning along the way, so they feel entitled to personal perspectives on the subject. To be perfectly frank, I felt the same way when I got into the business in my first year as a 4th grade teacher. However, when I got into Special Education, an uneasy ambivalence began to percolate through me. During my first two years as an elementary school teacher, I could rely on my knowledge of basic arithmetic, my ability to comprehend what I read as well as my skill in writing and spelling to see me through (although to this day, my spelling skill is barely adequate). I felt reasonably competent to guide and correct the average 4th-grader's academic development. For sure, there were a few other things that I had to bone-up on such as organizing the day, establishing routines, and redirecting counter-productive behaviour, but I had a grasp of what I needed, or at least what I thought I needed. In contrast, I found Special Education to be quite different. I knew from the outset it demanded a type of competence that I did not possess and, as stated in the previous chapter, one my formal preparation (i.e., my Special Education Certification) to that point in my emerging career, did little to fortify me for. But I was sure it was much more than *patience* that I needed.

Patience in teaching is often construed as one's ability to endure slow plodding advancement, or perhaps tolerate frequent regression in both academic and social/emotional development, calmly waiting for improvement to occur. The work of a few influential educators in the field helped me fend off such well-meaning references to *patience*. I'll forewarn readers that this chapter will dip into a kind of lecture-mode as I elaborate more on these influences, but I will reiterate that this memoir is not intended as a "how-to manual" even though it might appear to be heading in that direction. I feel readers will benefit from an understanding of the foundations of my practice as being skill-based and far from naturally occurring personality characteristics such as *patience*. I promise to be brief.

Effectiveness. That defines teaching. If children do not learn, there has been no teaching. The boldness in that statement was jaw-dropping for me when I first heard it back in the early 70s. I liked that assertion, but I must admit to being a bit skeptical when I heard Siegfried Engelmann[2] (more on him later in this chapter) excoriate the state of compensatory education in the US at the time when he sarcastically labeled ineffectiveness as "dysteachia". His complaint seemed to imply that the responsibility for ineffectiveness was solely the teacher's, and this appeared unfair to me. I felt there were too many variables that impinged on any teacher's ability to be *effective* in every set of circumstances, especially negative ones (e.g., inadequate curricular resources, a negative school culture, deleterious familial factors of the children, etc.). The assessments used to determine *effectiveness* didn't seem to account for the common obstacles children with disabilities have to overcome. Grade-level achievement using standardized tests is often used to account for *effectiveness*. The general population understand these measures and cling to them as evidence of "good" or "bad" instruction. I must confess to being a naïve disciple of this approach when I was first starting out. However, I gradually began to recognize standardized measures were woefully inadequate as measurement tools for children with disabilities. These tools were far too blunt to guide instruction. I needed more.

I became attracted to approaches that employed incremental measures of growth (i.e., Precision Teaching[3]). For example, instead of grade-level achievement scores for reading, I was trained to monitor the progress of sub-skills such as the types of decoding errors the children were making. I would track their frequency and chart daily progress to ensure troublesome error-types were coming down and not going up. Reading accuracy and reading rate (i.e., words read per minute) coupled to form a basis for the effectiveness (or ineffectiveness) of oral reading. Compare these two statements on a report card:

> Statement 1: *Isaac is currently reading at the 4th grade level, two years behind his peers. Although he is making gains, he struggles with more complicated comprehension exercises.*

> Statement 2: *Isaac is able to read 4th grade material at 150 words per minute. This reading rate is about the equivalent of natural speech. His decoding accuracy has improved from*

45% to 87% in this last reporting cycle. Subsequently, he is comprehending much more of what he reads. He has worked very hard to conquer his difficulties reading phonetically irregular words such as 'enough', and 'phone', and we find that his reliance on context clues has helped him anticipate these words far more accurately than a few months back. Currently his decoding errors are specific to the suffixes 'ed' and plural endings. His performance on reading comprehension is 100% for literal questions but slips down to 65% accuracy for inferential questions. His trajectory of growth suggests that he may be able to achieve age-appropriate levels of reading by the end of the year.

As a parent, which statement inspires more confidence as you assess the capacity of the teacher to help your son with his difficulties? Obviously, the second statement is superior, but it isn't just about parental communication. Measurement approaches such as *Precision Teaching* allowed me to adjust my instruction in a targeted manner. And it wasn't just *reading* that I was measuring. I applied this approach to mathematics, spelling, and expressive writing as well. Even classroom behaviour. Of course, statements like the one in Statement 2 would be supported by charts chronicling the progression of growth over time. Where appropriate, these charts were shared with the children as motivational enticements. Their learning would become more tangible to them. Data-based decision making was the key. I knew where my instruction was effective and where it wasn't. Thus, I could focus my efforts more strategically. In short, my practice felt more professional, and I was certain my *patience* was not contributing to that feeling.

Another skill I honed had nothing to do with content but had everything to do with *effectiveness*. In my first year of teaching, my Superintendent observed that I needed help (and rightly so) in understanding reinforcement. This sounds bland but it wasn't. In fact, my entry into the field of reinforcement was probably the single most beneficial influence of my career. Up to that point, I felt that if you encountered uncooperative behaviour, you called it out and punished the offending student. Something like, *Johnny, this is the second time you've interrupted the lesson. You'll have to sit out in the hall.* It didn't occur to me that I may have been encouraging Johnny's interruptions rather than discouraging them. I thought I was punishing him. Further to this, I also didn't realize I had to *teach* him prosocial behaviour, not just expect it. He needed to be taught this just as other children need to be taught to read or spell. I found this out when I attended a series of workshops led by psychologist Peter Lorimer from Thistledown Regional Centre, a treatment facility for children who exhibited significant aberrant behaviour, including children with autism. Lorimer introduced me (and others) to the proper execution of reinforcement strategies used in promoting prosocial behaviour. To my surprise, I had a lot of unlearning to do.

I'll be general here, but readers should know the judicious application of reinforcement strategies are very complex to orchestrate. Lorimer guided us in once-a-week workshop sessions for an entire term (about three months). The sessions were unlike anything I had experienced in a teaching/learning situation before. There were competencies you had to demonstrate, and mastery of each was a requirement for moving on. The assignments were classroom-based and thus useful in my day-to-day practice. I learned a lot more than what I will be able to share here, but I'll isolate a few components to illustrate the complexity inherent in the approach Lorimer was coaching us on.

Firstly, I learned that the definitions of reinforcement and punishment were dynamic rather than passive. This meant the definition of either one was determined not from their literal meaning but from their effect on the behaviour the teacher was promoting or trying to extinguish. Said differently, if a behaviour was observed to be stronger after you followed it with a consequence (e.g., praise or a scolding), it had been positively reinforced. If it weakened (i.e., got less frequent) it had been punished. So, the results of the consequence determined what had been done, not what was thought to be done. To illustrate this further, if you scolded a student (a consequence) for speaking out-of-turn, the student may appear to have responded by ceasing to blurt-out. But, if in another minute or so that same student spoke out-of-turn again, and again, each followed by another scolding, like it or not, the scolding was actually reinforcing the objectionable behaviour and not punishing it, even though a harsh scolding sounds punitive. Even banishing Johnny from the classroom might be rewarding to him, especially if he doesn't like what is going on in the classroom. Only the effect on his behaviour determines this. After about a dozen workshop sessions, I emerged completely transformed in how I managed redirection, and well-fortified with a new set of skills. Once I began to experience the power of these techniques, they became an essential component to my arsenal.

Returning to *patience*, a judicious orchestration of reinforcement strategies might be misconstrued as patience. It's an easy assumption to make. I will elaborate. One of the elements of reinforcement is *extinction*. Behavioural theory predicts if a behaviour goes unreinforced, it becomes extinct over time. This is *extinction*. I call it purposeful ignoring. This means if Jane blurts out-of-turn, and I ignore her and continue to ignore her as if Jane were not there, eventually Jane's objectionable behaviour should diminish, assuming of course, she wanted my attention. The strategy usually has to be coupled with a *catching-the-kid-doing-something-good* approach. Thus, when I eventually see Jane's hand pop up, I can acknowledge it. *Yes Jane. I liked the way you put your hand up before answering.* To the uninitiated, the ignoring part in *catching-the-kid-doing-something-good* may look like nothing more than *patience* when, in fact, it was much more than that (i.e., purposeful ignoring to seed an appropriate response through positive reinforcement). For more troublesome cases, a teacher might have to add another component. To illustrate this technique: if Jane is not responding to my ignoring and continues to blurt out-of-turn, I might employ a *lever*. Levers work in the following way. I would gushingly reinforce Sally (sitting beside Jane) who happens to have her hand up waiting to offer an answer. *Sally. I like the way you are putting your hand up before answering.* Sally might not need the praise, but it nudges Jane toward understanding what she has to do without giving her any attention. My experience has taught me that troubled children often don't desire teacher-attention as much as they want to siphon it away from others. If a teacher conditions the student to expect their attention only through appropriate classroom behaviour, then the student begins to generalize this as a norm that must be honoured. Granted, the approach is subtle and out of view to most, but enormously effective in promoting prosocial behaviour. However, learning to trust these techniques takes time and a steadfast adherence to the principles of reinforcement as well as continual objective appraisal of one's effectiveness. One must be constantly vigilant. Patience won't get you there.

There is much more to reinforcement strategies of course. For example, there are schedules of reinforcement, secondary reinforcement through token economies, and the fading of reinforcement—all necessary in affecting enduring behaviour-change. But to what end? To achieve behavioural control? Sounds Machiavellian. This is the part that goes well beyond the gaze of the naïve onlooker. The goal in any behavioural-change approach should be to achieve reliable prosocial behaviour in the absence of reinforcement. In other words, for children to regulate their own behaviour so they are better able to attend to academics. When this is achieved, the teacher has accomplished a great thing. The child feels a healthier sense of belonging by modulating their own behaviour in synchrony with the norms of the group. Because of this, stronger instructional engagement is achieved and, if the instruction is good, a surge of self-confidence from the learning they are experiencing ensues. In this way, prosocial behaviour is taught, not just managed. Again, patience can not accomplish this.

There is a catch to all this, which is the need for classroom management techniques to be coupled with high quality curricula. Adequate prosocial behaviour is more likely to persist when it is partnered with well-designed curricula. In the field of general education, high quality curricula abound. Sadly, in the field of Special Education, it is scarcer. This brings me to another rich influence in my career. During Lorimer's workshops he kept stressing the need for having a powerful curriculum, one that is well suited to the special needs of children who have enormous challenges to their learning. He introduced us to Direct Instruction (DI)[4]. Siegfried Engelmann was the principal author of this program. He was an interesting character. He was from the University of Oregon in Eugene. I had the pleasure of meeting him a couple of times. Engelmann was a tall, lugubrious sort, who wore crumpled clothes and a poor fitting tie. He had long arms with outsized hands that would be in constant motion when he talked. Inspirational would not be a term you would apply to him at first glance. However, his driving irreverence pulled me in. He was angry about what he called *dysteachia*. He scoffed at labels such as *dyslexic* and *learning disabilities*. For him, these children were simply casualties of poor teaching. He chastised the teaching profession for failing children who struggled. He'd waive his long arms around in angry displays, castigating the state of modern education in its inadequate service for impoverished communities. I can still recall him shouting out, "Get the hook!" This was his crass way of saying, *if you can't teach, get out of the classroom.* It was refreshing to hear, but I will admit to feeling intimidated by the challenge.

Engelmann did not start out as an educator. But he became a very good one, and his reputation for working with very difficult children was held in high regard. He and his colleague, Wesley Becker, were obsessed with instructional effectiveness. Embodied in DI were language efficiencies called *scripted formats*. Teachers were trained to use instructional language in very specific ways: when introducing a topic, for practicing a skill, and for correcting students when they made errors. Engelmann and Becker observed that instructional language was where teachers' pedagogical effectiveness usually failed, especially with disadvantaged learners. Subsequently, they studied where ambiguity seeped into teachers' instructional language and they prescribed alternative wording (i.e., *scripted formats* similar to actors learning lines in a play). They also recognized that conventional curricula lacked an emphasis on the mastery of readiness skills—prerequisite skills necessary for more advanced learning. They felt typical curricula advanced far too abruptly for disadvantaged learners. Mastery was the goal of every lesson, and students did not move on until it was achieved. I'll add a subtle point here that became a profound discovery for me. When the struggling learner is just beginning to resolve their difficulties, it is not the lesson content that motivates them. Rather, it is their perception of their emerging competence. Their oral reading begins to resemble natural speech: their spelling, their mathematics calculations—everything becomes more automatic. They sense the change and enjoy demonstrating their newly discovered fluency. That is why they can practice skills that are, in the beginning at least, not inherently interesting to them. With the advent of improved fluency teachers can begin to integrate content knowledge to the curriculum (i.e., reading to learn as opposed to learning to read).

The DI curricula he and his colleagues developed, addressed oral language, early reading, spelling, and mathematics. Later, he introduced DI for comprehension and critical thinking. Their approach was such a departure from conventional approaches that it encountered considerable criticism. Engelmann was not shy about defending his programs, nor did he back away from criticizing other programs if their effectiveness could not be demonstrated. His mantra was always *effectiveness*. If an approach was promoted as being effective, then prove it. The adversity he created came to a head in 1969 when the results from Project Follow Through were published. Project Follow Through was the largest national investigation of effectiveness ever conducted in the US. All the major approaches to teaching disadvantaged learners were evaluated. DI emerged with significantly stronger outcomes than all the others on every measure. People took notice. They had no choice.

I undertook some DI training, knowing that it was what I needed in my Special Education classroom. As with the reinforcement training I received with Peter Lorimer, DI training was equally rigorous. You were taught, coached, and evaluated by trained DI professionals. I liked this. There was an undeniable level of technical skill required to be an effective DI teacher. Watching a proficient DI lesson was something to behold. Students were engaged, the learning was obvious, and the students' self-confidence was tangible. Better still, DI teachers could be successful with even the most challenging students. I wanted to be like that.

Underlying DI was the notion that any child could be taught, regardless of their disability. This assumes the instruction was appropriate and well executed. Admittedly, this seemed a bit utopian, and I had my doubts. I felt I was having remarkable success with some students, but not all of them. There were still certain instances where DI approaches did not seem to be enough.

This brings me to one additional, but important, influence. My career was leading me more and more into the area of emotional disturbance (ED). Often these children had only mild academic difficulties. Their primary challenge extended from their inability to self-regulate in social settings. Violent outbursts, confrontational reactions, deceitfulness, excessive egocentricity, coarse language, and a host of other anti-social conduct often characterized these students' behaviours. This negative conduct interfered with classroom expectations and their academic progress. Usually, but not always, children with ED came from abusive backgrounds. Some experienced profound neglect or unspeakable tragedy. Some encountered both. They were quite damaged emotionally and had very little personal or social resources to draw upon. My knowledge of reinforcement strategies and curricular design was helpful in many ways, but I recognized these skills were not sufficient to be effective with youngsters with ED. I knew I needed something more. Fritz Redl and David Wineman published a couple of books that provided much needed guidance for me. *Controls from Within: Techniques for the Treatment of the Aggressive Child*[5] and *Children Who Hate*[6] offered clinical techniques for shepherding students through intense emotional episodes to bring them back to a state of equilibrium. A more contemporary application of Redl and Wineman's approach was formalized as *Life Space Crisis Intervention*[7] by Nicholas Long and William Morse. These authors employed mental hygienic language in their de-escalation techniques. Transcripts of behavioural therapists navigating through the various stages of an emotional breakdown were used to illustrate the path taken to return the student to a level of self-regulation. There was a reasoned progression to this language that I found compelling. When used appropriately, students with ED became more emotionally stable and thus more teachable. It taught them self-regulation as opposed to just the teacher controlling them.

It served another function as well, one I found to be even more important when working with children with ED. The approach also helped me control my own emotions while executing de-escalation techniques. During such episodes, teachers are often unwittingly drawn into the emotional fray. They may get hijacked by their own tempers and conduct themselves in imprudent ways; ways that are anything but mentally hygienic. Teachers may shout in anger, punish excessively, or become paralyzed from the intensity of the moment and cease to act in a way that will return the classroom back to a state of equilibrium.

Mental hygienic approaches allowed me to visualize the offending student as a *victim* of their circumstances and less as a *villain*. This simple switch in perspective, ensured a stronger altruistic orientation. It was a way to depersonalize the event and stay objective. A second benefit to the approach was it gave me a map to navigate my way back to equilibrium without the child experiencing any loss in self-esteem. Knowing where you are in an episode of deregulation (escalation or de-escalation stages) and where you are heading is so important in situations like these. If the child is raging out of control to the point where they must be restrained for their own safety and the safety of others (including me), there was comfort in knowing the steps needed to remedy the situation. I refer to it as "knowing the way back"; back to where order, predictability, and psychological safety reside. Watching very troubled children return to these islands of psychological safety time and time again, provided me with great satisfaction.

Returning to *patience* one last time. Over the years, I have been observed teaching in many difficult Special Education settings. I have had student teachers, visiting teachers, parents, and administrators watch me in the classroom and in clinical situations. As I write this, I am cringing from the boastful language I am using. I apologize but persist shamelessly, nonetheless. On these occasions, the observers provided me with accolades. Their comments may have pertained to observed efficiencies, robust student engagement, or an abundance of self-regulated, prosocial behaviour. Perhaps more. However, I would not allow any of those accolades to include the word *patience* without challenging it. I might add, there were days when any visitor to my classroom would not be impressed at all. And on those days, my skill set was probably only a tiny bit better than the most novice teacher. But when I was on my game, I was proud—proud that I had mastered a set of skills non-teachers didn't have and ones many experienced teachers couldn't lay claim to. I felt I had achieved this through my own initiative, not my patience.

Chapter 5: Kmart and Beer Labels

One of the most intriguing conditions experienced in schools is autism. Throughout my career, I have had three students on the autism spectrum as part of my work as a Special Education teacher. In addition, I directed a camp for individuals with autism serving approximately forty campers, ages 5 to 21. In total, I believe I have had more exposure to this condition than most Special Educators experience in a lifetime of community schooling. I witnessed firsthand the range of characteristics that individuals with autism display, and more importantly, I had many immersive interactions with their families that brought me in touch with the enormity of their everyday challenges.

Individuals on the autistic spectrum can range from severely developmentally disadvantaged to uniquely capable[8]. Proportioning the spectrum into the different subgroups is confounded by the variability in criteria used in the identification process as well as with the appropriateness of the measures employed (e.g., appropriateness of language-based IQ tests for a population whose abilities with language are compromised). Also, their developmental trajectories can be influenced by intervention strategies used to educate them. However, there is no "cure" in the sense that the manifestation of the disorder disappears over time even with therapy. Symptoms may moderate but not cease. Individuals with autism often present with cognitive anomalies that make the functional aspects of daily life both challenging for them and for those that care for them. Their symptoms can isolate them as being unusual in obvious ways such as a lack of eye-contact, a prevalence of ritualized obsessions, and a predilection for social isolation. For many, an autistic child's insistence for order and predictability (this can often be extreme) ensures an added level of stress for the family as they attempt to organize their lives around their child's obsessions. Energy-depleting tantrums can ensue. This is especially true for families who have other children's needs to manage as well as their autistic child's.

The characteristics of this syndrome are interesting enough on their own, but when the disorder manifests itself as savant-like as in the movie, *Rain Man* starring Dustin Hoffman, the level of intrigue rises considerably. The prevalence of autistic savants is very rare, perhaps one in a million. These individuals can have remarkable splinter skills in areas like music or calculating yet be severely delayed in other important functional areas. Kenny was one of those children.

Kenny's family moved to the school where I worked at mid-year. He came from a large family. Kenny would have been about 10 years old at the time. I can recall him being third in age with two younger siblings and two older, one or both of whom were teenagers. The family left a remote fishing village in northeastern Newfoundland and moved from there to a bustling metropolitan area outside of Toronto. I could not imagine a more striking contrast in terms of community characteristics. The arrival of the family at our school was a bit of a jolt, partly due to the size of the family as well as their choice to move in the middle of the year. But Kenny dramatically increased the level of complication for us. Kenny had never attended school! This set off alarm bells. From the outset, it was obvious there was something very unusual about him that made the possibility of a regular grade-level placement completely out of the question. He not only exhibited the classic signs of autism, but he also appeared to have savant-like characteristics.

About that time (in the mid-1970s), autism was a rare occurrence in community schools and autistic savants were found only in publications that sensationalized their abilities. Right from the outset, Kenny garnered much attention. As with many children with autism, he presented with little spontaneous language. Gestures and one-word requests (e.g., thirsty, bathroom, etc.) constituted the extent of his expressive language. Although he could not engage in conversation, he seemed to understand simple requests, such as *back to your seat* or *get your coat*. He was a cute little child, quite unremarkable in many ways, but his gaze pulled you in. It imbued intense curiosity, angled off to the side, while he blinked incessantly as if trying to focus on something just beyond his view. That, and persistent hand-flapping made him stand out from his same-aged peers.

His savant characteristics were remarkable. I will share some examples. Upon his initial enrollment, his mother claimed that he could read. I must admit to being a bit doubtful about this assertion right from the beginning since he didn't seem to have any oral language, but something happened that made me realize what she had meant. On occasion, Kenny would mimic reading but not actually perform the function of reading (i.e., decoding text to generate meaning). I discovered this quite by accident. I will caution readers that the threads of my memory begin to fray a bit as I reconstruct this account, so I will keep it general. One day, Kenny spontaneously recited a large chunk of text, probably a few paragraphs in length. It was impressive, especially knowing that up to that point all he would utter was one-word expressions of need. Nothing more. I do not recall exactly what prompted the sudden recitation. He may have overheard some reading being done in one of the other instructional groups in the classroom, or the piece may have been overheard while one of his older siblings wrestled with a homework assignment. Quite out of the blue, he began verbalizing an uninterrupted flow of sentences without the benefit of text. The passage was long enough to challenge most anyone's ability to memorize. However, he was able to do it, seemingly with no effort at all. Let me reiterate, this was purely an oral exercise, not reading. He was simply mimicking what he had heard somewhere, perhaps just once. And why this passage, I could not say, as efforts to get him to recite other passages read to him failed. It seemed that he had to latch onto something on his own. It was shocking, but I could see how his mother may have confused this ability with actual reading. Later, I observed a similarly awe-inspiring ability. Kenny liked to draw a single comic-book scene from his favourite cartoon show, *The Flintstones*. While drawing the caricatures depicted in the cartoon, he would mimic the dialogue as he drew, parrot-like, complete with different voices and vocal inflections. This was a rote activity though, as there was no indication that he was either enjoying the humour or associating with the narrative flow, yet there was something mysterious that fed this impulse, again and again—the same scene, caught in the spin-cycle of his mind, endlessly fascinating him for reasons unknown.

He would draw anytime he could and his ability to capture the specific details of an image was astounding. However, he was not an artist. His renderings were limited to Kmart signs, beer labels and the one *Flintstones* scene. Nothing else. But they were perfect in every way. The colour, the proportion, and the detail, all without the benefit of a visual image to copy from. He could do this all day long if allowed. The content of his drawings raised a few questions. Why K-Mart and why beer labels? In conversation with his family, I found out that Kenny's bedroom in Newfoundland, the place where he spent most of his day, overlooked a beer depot where returns were stored. Boxes upon boxes would be piled up just outside his window waiting to be returned to the brewery. Together they formed a small mountain of patterns for him to perseverate on. There was something compelling in those logos that he latched onto. As for the Kmart logo, his mother reported Kenny's obsession with the weekly sale flyer appearing on their doorstep. He'd play with the flyer with as much rapture as a typical child would with a new toy. Whatever the catalyst was for these images, they etched on his mind and became the sole subject of his artwork. These and the *Flintstones* characters.

His drawing process would consist of much stopping and starting, pausing to look up and off to the side, blinking all the while. His pauses could last for several minutes. Then he would continue to draw where he left off. His face did not always focus directly on the image he was creating, yet he was able to draw with machine-like precision as if he was tracing over an image, one that was guiding his hand. His renderings were good, yet if he were asked to draw something specific—a tree, a flower, or a sketch of a person—he either wouldn't or couldn't. I was never sure which.

Getting back to Kenny's education, it was clear that Kenny needed a lot more than I was able to give him. Improving his spontaneous language was first and foremost in his development, but it was clear the type of programming he needed could not be supplied in the setting he now found himself. The school psychologist, in consultation with his parents, made a referral to a specialized facility where Kenny could be properly assessed. In the meantime, I did what I could. After the first few months, something interesting began happening that was not planned for. Kenny's cuteness endeared him to others and there was always a group of older kids (usually girls) that would come and get him at recess. I remember being worried that they were treating him like a toddler, perhaps becoming overly involved in helping him. I thought he should become more independent and felt the girls may be doing too much for him. I would go out in the school yard to monitor the situation. I saw them including him in their games. Games like dodgeball, skipping, and hopscotch were regular activities in the playground, and Kenny was made a part of it but in a highly prompted way. Any joy stemming from spontaneous play was not apparent as he mindlessly participated as if he were one of their dolls. Somehow though, he seemed to be integrating into the microculture of schoolyard activities. This was puzzling, as I wasn't sure it was true behaviour-change or a re-emergence of behaviours that were dormant while he adjusted to his new surroundings. In class, I began noticing other subtle changes as well. His eye-contact became more centred, the blinking less apparent. He began using phrases in his spontaneous speech instead of the one-word blurt-outs that dominated his speech when he first arrived. It was as if he was absorbing social interaction osmotically. But here is the interesting part: while all this was happening, his obsessive drawing ceased to occupy him as it once did. Pencil crayons and drawing paper remained untouched for days on end, a remarkable change from his usual obsession. More mysteriously, these positive changes were occurring without any specific interventions on my part.

This apparent growth was very encouraging, but he remained a ten-year-old boy who was far from typical. He needed much more. It may have been two or three months before Kenny's referral to the autism clinic was arranged. I am not sure how it came to be, but I remember accompanying the family to the centre. The centre was in another city, about two hours away. Perhaps they didn't have a car, necessitating my involvement. Perhaps they wanted someone there, someone they knew and trusted. Perhaps the centre needed my input as I was his teacher. It might have been all three for that matter. I can't recall the reason, but I do remember going with them.

His parents had been made aware that should the clinic find Kenny eligible for treatment, he could, if they wished, reside there for his treatment. They were also made aware it might take a couple of years before Kenny's treatment goals were met. His parents were understandably anxious. When the session ended, they were told Kenny would be a good candidate for the program. The news gnawed at them during the lengthy ride home, and I became an unwitting facilitator in their deliberation. They were a simple family dealing with an enormously complex problem. And to be fair, autism was not well-understood by the professional community at that time (mid 1970s). Worse even, some damaging perspectives had been postulated a few years prior. Bruno Bettelheim, for example, placed most of autism's etiology on failings of parents, suggesting the children's perpetual aloneness stemmed from inadequate caring of some kind or another. The term *refrigerator mothers* was associated with his theoretical framework, caustically implying a lack of warmth from the mother was the problem. When Kenny was being evaluated, the field was still struggling to shed the negative implications of these disparaging perspectives on parenting[9]. It is highly probable Kenny's parents would have known nothing of this debate, but they did not need convincing that Kenny's communication needs were significant, and these needs seemed to be well beyond the ability of a community school to rectify. But as I reflect on this now, the decision was essentially one of blind trust—accepting the recommendation from knowledgeable professionals who claimed they had answers, but the parents not knowing enough to challenge the veracity of the professionals' judgement. They did, however, know one thing better than the professionals. They knew about their son and what he needed from his family. It was a deep and abiding feeling that only parents can feel, one that could, and perhaps should, override scientific certitude. They may have felt the anticipated benefits promoted in the specialized program might not warrant the temporary severing of the family bond with their child. The Speech and Language Pathologists who completed the assessment that day may have been only able to see the autism. His parents, on the other hand, were aware of something far more compelling—his complete dependence on them, the tug of their nurturance unyielding. They may have been worried less about the deficiencies identified in the assessment and more about making things worse for him (and for them). He wasn't a project to them; he was their fragile little boy. It was risky.

In the end, they decided Kenny should go. I imagine this is where my perspective on delivering professional advice began to mature. Over the years, I have learned when professional advice is given to parents, whether it be good advice or bad, the parents are the only ones that will have to live through the consequences of that advice. In my experience, parents know their own reality well. They know their strengths and limitations, and this knowledge gives them legitimacy in weighing the merits of a recommendation against their personal circumstances. The value of any advice must bow reverentially to their reality, and not just the reality as described by the professionals. This became a major tenet for me as I consulted with parents over the years. Later in my career, I was able to share this perspective with student teachers, knowing perhaps, their nascent perspectives may one day compete with parental concerns, naïvely perceiving perhaps, these concerns as somehow less worthy than their professional judgement.

I don't know what happened to Kenny the months after he left the school for the clinic. I was transferred to another school at the end of that year. I often think of Kenny when I see an adult on the street who appears to be autistic and wonder if it could be him. Since that time with Kenny and his family, some very promising results have come from early-intervention techniques now available to most communities. Techniques such as Applied Behavioural Analysis[10] have focused on replacing maladaptive behaviours with more functionally adaptive ones. This has made a tremendous difference in the lives of many children with autism and their families. I like to think that Kenny may have received that kind of help early enough to have made a substantial difference in his life. But I also know there are no silver bullets in this business.

The horizon for most of these children and their families is usually limited. I had mentioned in the introduction to this chapter that I once directed a camp for individuals with autism. In this camp, I had older campers (ages 18 to 21) whose functional levels were very low, and the burden of their need for continual care was apparent to anyone who worked with them. It seemed to me they had reached an impassable ceiling in their development. This was an abhorrent thought but a reality, nonetheless. This limitation was made abundantly clear to me one day, quite by accident. Approximately five years after directing the camp, I attended a conference sponsored by the Council for Exceptional Children. I went to hear a presentation from a distinguished scholar about a method for engaging children with autism. Included in the presenter's speech was some older video footage of children who used to attend her clinic. The video was demonstrating the technique she was pioneering. To my astonishment, the children in the video happened to include four or five of the children I had in my camp, only instead of being 18 or 19 as I knew them, they were 12 or 13. What was fascinating to me was they seemed to be the same in almost every respect except size. In other words, they had not developed in any discernable way in terms of language usage or in their classic autistic behaviours in the five years of development that preceded my involvement with them. Those in the audience surely did not know this, and they might have wrongly assumed these children were on a trajectory of continual growth. The years ahead of them may have looked promising, more promising than they actually were. This was certainly the message implied by the presenter. Unfortunately for the subjects in the video, my experience with these same children as 18- and 19-year-olds was far less optimistic. It was clear to me they had either plateaued or had regressed, and they were nothing more than older versions of the same children captured in the video. They would be the *vanquished* in the perceptual categories I have used to structure this memoir. Unfortunately, vanquishment is an unavoidable perception faced by many parents, teachers, and even children with disabilities. This is no truer than for those who serve families dealing with autism. A parent's hope for continual improvement can often sputter and become extinguished, snuffed out by the mysterious neurology that perpetuates the troubling peculiarities of their children's autism. Acceptance is what they have been left with. That, and the horror of knowing their child's need for continual support will likely outlive them. This is not the case for every family of course, but I suspect it is for most.

Chapter 6: Encopresis (a.k.a. Poop)

Self-harm. We see it in schools. It is mostly benign—students who hand in an incomplete assignment and incur a lower grade, or they break a school rule and must endure an unpleasant detention. It ramps up a bit when we see young teenagers carving up their skin or denying themselves proper nutrition such as with anorexia. When we witness these behaviours, we often scratch our heads and wonder why they do these kinds of things to themselves. Life would be a lot easier for them if they didn't, right? Patrick had one of these perplexing kinds of problems. He was in 8th grade and normal in every respect, except one. He was encopretic—he soiled himself, often. I became involved with Patrick's case while serving as a Special Educator in his school. Patrick was a low-average student, but his school progress was not considered low enough to qualify him for Special Education, at least under an academic criterion. Instead, his condition necessitated tertiary Special Education involvement to help him conquer his encopresis.

Patrick was new to the school, coming from another jurisdiction. He had recently been adopted by his aunt, following the death of his birth mother. She (his birth mother) had a protracted illness that affected Patrick deeply. I can not recall the full story of his early childhood, especially the role of his biological father, but I do remember some details. We learned that Patrick's father left the family unit soon after Patrick's birth mother was diagnosed with her illness. There were rumours of psychological abuse perpetrated by the father and it was suggested to us that Patrick's encopresis may have been exacerbated by an anxiety response, possibly due to abuse. A psychological report attesting to this might have contributed to this idea, but my memory is fuzzy here. I do remember, however, that Patrick's bowel problems had been with him before he arrived at our school. Patrick's aunt and his cousin Cory (his newly adoptive family) had their own challenges. She was a single mother trying to do her best on a meagre income. Her biological son Cory, also in 8th grade, was already a student in our school and was receiving Special Education programing (from me) for mild cognitive disabilities. Cory found school challenging both academically and socially. The added stress of his new brother's encopresis probably didn't help.

What to do? Sorting through the causes and isolating the possible psychological ones from the physical ones seemed important. Previous medical examinations revealed that Patrick was capable of normal bowel function and his physiology did not appear to be contributing to his encopresis. With physiological causes in doubt, I focused on his behavioural habits. Here's where I will invoke two of the 3-Vs, *victim* and *villain*. In normal development, children learn to interpret body signals and activate appropriate toileting behaviour in response to these signals. Patrick was well past the age where a failure to respond to the signals was excusable. Either Patrick's signals were being interrupted, or there was something reinforcing Patrick's aversion to proper toileting that I did not understand. Many years later, I am able to recognize my approach pushed and pulled at these two perceptual dichotomies—were there psychological stressors beyond his ability to control (i.e., he was a victim), or was there some kind of pathological motive at play, a willful apathy perhaps, purposely arousing the angst of those around him (i.e., he was a villain)?

His classmates, understandably, viewed his condition with little sympathy. Uncharitable derision, often overt, accompanied "accidents" when they occurred. The smell was offensive, and he would be ostracised by them. Their perception, it would seem, tilted toward *villain*. If you viewed his problem as being within his control, one might ask: *Doesn't he see what he is doing to himself?* Frustration, anger, or scorn ensued—all negative. On the other hand, if you were able to view the problem differently, one that concluded the accidents were outside of his direct control, you might ask a different question: *What things in his environment are exacerbating his condition?* Here, more adaptive responses might result—all positive. I must confess to holding the former view as opposed to the latter. In my defense, I was young (I was in my fifth or sixth year) at the time, and my perspective on disabling conditions such as Patrick's had not evolved much.

I'll illustrate how my approach to Patrick's problem manifested itself early on. I was in my classroom working with a few children when Jerome, the custodian, came and called me out of the room. He wanted to alert me to the feces in the hall. He reported he had been sweeping when he noticed the excrement drop right out of Patrick's pants and on to the floor. Patrick had been standing in line with his classmates waiting for the other class to clear the gym. Jerome was understandably startled. Patrick either didn't seem to notice or didn't appear to care. I called Patrick out of the gym and showed him the feces. I felt the evidence was irrefutable and the obviousness of it would jolt him into reality. He claimed it could not have been him! How could he claim innocence? I questioned him further and asked him if he noticed his clothes smelled. He denied smelling anything. He didn't appear arrogant or defensive in any particular way. In fact, he seemed so thoroughly convinced that it wasn't him, I really had to reconsider what I was dealing with. Was it an intentional denial to avoid blame? Or did he experience some kind of psychological blocking to help him deal with the shame he was feeling or, perhaps, should be feeling? I cannot think of a more embarrassing moment for a teenager to endure than to incur a dreaded accident in full view of one's classmates. The social harm he was doing to himself was inexplicable, and my insistence he recognize this reality did little to advance a positive solution to his problem. At times, I had to restrain the impulse to scold him.

As the school year progressed, Patrick's encopresis gradually improved. This was probably due, in part, to the intervention that was provided at school, but it was equally likely there were other beneficial factors involved (e.g., his grief from his birth mother's death subsiding). The intervention consisted of the following. The school did not have a shower but there was private toilet in the furnace room that Jerome offered. His adoptive mother compiled a kit for him to clean himself up and a change of clothes was supplied that could be left in the furnace room. His mother was asked to treat accidents as matter-of-factly as she could when he arrived home with soiled clothing—no punishment or shaming. As an alternative, his consequence was that he was charged with the responsibility of cleaning his own clothes and supplying properly laundered replacements for the ones used at school. I arranged with his teachers that he could leave the classroom at any time without seeking their permission in order to attend to his toileting needs. It was important to have as little attention directed toward him as possible. We also felt we could not make him responsible for cleaning up his mess should there be some, fearing that this might aggravate any psychological stress he may be feeling, especially if his classmates were around to see it. Jerome, God bless him. I can recall him saying, "I clean vomit up regularly, why wouldn't I clean poop up." Eventually, Patrick was able to intercept an accident from happening and was able to make it to the toilet before one occurred. By the end of the year, he was accident-free.

Later in my career (about 35 years later), I was teaching a course entitled, Introduction to Emotional Disturbance, to a group of student teachers. We were discussing encopresis and enuresis as a topic, and I was using Patrick's case as an example. I invited a clinic colleague as a guest. He was a psychologist who specialized in toileting issues. I thought that when I shared my observation that Patrick was in 8th grade, it would surprise him. It didn't. I thought that my observation that Patrick was seemingly without shame would shock him. It didn't. I thought that Patrick's apparent failure to notice both the discomfort of sitting in soiled clothes and the smell emanating around him would challenge my colleague's comprehension beyond the limits of common credence. Again, it didn't. I was astounded! I desperately wanted the reasons for Patrick's encopresis to be wildly Freudian. I could sense the intrigue in my students. It was palpable. I didn't want them to be disappointed. But my colleague didn't bite. Instead, he claimed that cases like Patrick's can be so severe that the children often simply habituate to their condition to the point where they don't even recognize the problem. He likened it to the anesthesia received in the dentist chair, *You know someone is inflicting great pain on you, pain you will feel most profoundly when the anesthetic wears off, yet you are able to suspend it.* He claimed that is how habituation works. The source of Patrick's problem was as uninteresting as a trip to the dentist, and given how it ended, my colleague was probably correct.

I would like to be able to state that my approach was based on sound psychological principles, but I would be wrong. I was guessing. A common-sense approach turned out to be the best one. Retrospectively however, I can see how important it was to avoid the "shame game". Addressing the problem with harsh reality checks may have only exacerbated the problem further. Treating it as a relearning problem instead, allowed Patrick's development to catch up to where it should have been in the first place, without the lingering scars of shame. Although I can't be completely sure of this, Patrick probably carried a fragment of psychological stress into his adult years. How could he not? The damage was done, but he had found a way to adapt, making his condition less debilitating, possibly furthering opportunities for positive social interactions as he matured into adulthood.

Cases like Patrick's reinforce the importance of managing one's perception-forming tendencies. Being quick to render judgement is rarely helpful and, in Patrick's case, probably harmful. One must resist the temptation to assume there is always a wilfulness behind objectionable behaviour. Quite often, the root causes are quite a bit more obscure, and the offending student's motives are driven not by evil, but by the confluence of many tertiary forces that impinge on the student's conscious and unconscious behaviour—forces not under the direct influence of the child. In these kinds of cases, I found it much more helpful to assume non-volitional motives behind the behaviours—*victim* instead of *villain*. Of course, one could always be wrong. Evil does exist. But, in my experience with many troubled children, it is exceedingly rare.

Chapter 7: Rage

"He died suddenly"—a phrase often seen in obituaries. These three words bulge with implication, particularly if the deceased is young. You think drug overdose or suicide right away. Maybe a violent death. Bad stuff. I encountered this phrase when I stumbled on Calvin's obituary while preparing to write this chapter. Calvin had been a student of mine in the early 80s. Many years after Calvin left my program, I accidentally bumped into his father in a grocery store. When the conversation turned to Calvin, he mentioned he had committed a severe crime a few years after leaving high school and was serving time in jail. Thinking Calvin would be a good candidate for this topic, I wanted to see if I could find some archival information on the incident to include in this chapter. Instead, I found his obituary. It contained the dreaded phrase, *he died suddenly*. There was no statement explaining the circumstances, just: "he died suddenly." What had happened that led to this? He was 49.

You hit your thumb with a hammer, you get caught in a traffic jam, or you incur an insult; rage ensues. It is natural, and we all experience it at various levels. It may even be considered an adaptive response to aversive stimuli (e.g., when being attacked by a wild animal or an archenemy). However, when it is unchecked or poorly managed, it usually becomes a social problem. Worse still, when it occurs with little or no provocation, there is likely an underlying psychological disturbance behind it. This applied to Calvin.

Freckle-faced, with an engaging smile, Calvin had a beguiling charm that drew you in. His easy presence belied an undercurrent of rage that boiled just below the surface. He would have been about 10 years old when he was enrolled in my class for children with emotional disturbances (ED). It was a special class that had been set up for children who had difficulty with emotional regulation. He had been referred to the program after he was deemed unmanageable by his regular elementary school. His file was thick with incident reports involving physical altercations with classmates and teachers. On a few occasions, police were involved.

His family background is a factor in this story, but I will caution readers to think of Calvin's problems as being multi-faceted, including some psychotic tendencies. Still, I can't deny there were negative forces at play in the family dynamic. However, his family, such as it was, remained a source of support for Calvin during the time I was involved with him. His father was a recovering alcoholic who fell off the wagon periodically. Unfortunately, when this happened, he would become physically and emotionally abusive to Calvin's mother. Calvin and his two brothers (Calvin was the middle child) would have witnessed some of this abuse, but I was not aware any of them were being abused, at least physically that is. I will add that when Calvin's father was sober, he was as engaged in his children's lives as most any other father would have been. He coached Calvin's soccer team and he was an avid supporter at Calvin's hockey games. When he was sober, I was pleased to have him in the classroom every couple of weeks to teach the students how to play chess. I felt it would be good for Calvin to see his father in a positive light and for me to see how the two of them interacted.

I'll digress to explain how my involvement with students like Calvin came to be. About ten years into my career, I became focused on students with ED. Childhood rage is often a prevalent characteristic of these children. Over the years, I had the good fortune to observe a few excellent mental health professionals. I was intrigued at how competent they were in handling difficult situations. I wanted to learn more, especially how to deal with rage.

To those who are unfamiliar with ED classrooms, the role of an educator in a rage episode may look like it has wandered far from the traditional role of teacher—one whose primary purpose is to engage children in academic growth. Consider this situation: walking by a classroom door and seeing the teacher physically restraining a furious child, in amongst the wreckage of an overturned couple of desks, while the child in question is spewing the vilest invective imaginable at the teacher and their classmates. It's not what you'd expect to see a teacher doing, right? But situations like this could be encountered regularly in an ED classroom.

A rage episode has layers to it, and each has its own level of complexity. I have learned that therapeutic responses to rage require a unique set of skills that are appropriate for every layer. One must know what they are doing to return the situation to a state of equilibrium. I took great pride in executing some of these skills, yet I never felt this skill set was completely understood by either my superiors or by some of my less-informed colleagues. To address this, I formalized the approach into a program called *Victimless Teaching* (VT), one that was built upon a strong theoretical base. The following is a summary of this approach.

A central tenet of VT is that the teacher manages their own perceptions. As mentioned previously, this is not a switch you turn on and off but rather an attempt to harness your assumptions about the wilfulness of the raging child. It is based on the principle that it is easier to offer a therapeutic response to a rage episode when the child is viewed more as a *victim* than a *villain*—a victim of circumstances outside of the child's control as opposed to being perceived as a villain, operating with wilful maliciousness. To illustrate this, consider your reaction to being bumped from behind while standing in line. This might arouse one's annoyance until you turn and see that the offending person has dark glasses and a white cane. Any negative feelings begin to drain away as the assumptions of villainy evaporate—the person was blind and couldn't have known you were there. There was no malice intended here. VT relies on this perceptual shift. One must look beyond the episode being experienced to the psychological roots driving the rage. This is not easy when you are embroiled in a conflict but terribly important, nonetheless. If one doesn't (or isn't able to) attend to this perceptual adjustment, feelings of retribution can inadvertently engage negative responses to such episodes. This may sound a bit "touchy-feely", but I have found excessive punishment can diminish the opportunity for therapeutic gain. To be clear, I am not advocating for the removal of punishment as a tool in shaping behaviour but rather deemphasizing its power to evoke change. Here is an example of what I mean. I once had an out-of-control child bite my hand as I tried to prevent him from hurting another child. When discussing a possible punishment for this with a seasoned Youth Care worker assisting me, she rightly asked, "What are you going to do to him that hasn't already been done?" It was one of those gravity-inducing questions. The youngster in question had a history replete with abuse. He had been burned by an enraged parent. Hideous scars from the incident defaced his cheek and neck, reminders of the atrocities wrecked on this child. She was correct. As much as I may have wanted him to "pay" for injuring my hand, I knew there was no punishment I could conjure up that would trump what had already been done to him. He was clearly a *victim* and not a *villain*. For many children with ED, there are no visible scars to remind you of their victimhood. But that doesn't mean the scars are not still there, hidden from view perhaps, but still driving the rage. Punishment is a weak antidote for these children. Other tools are needed if self-regulation is the goal.

Back to the layers of a rage episode. The first layer is de-escalation. Preventing an episode from escalating to rage is the most useful skill one can possess. Unfortunately, it is not always possible with children with ED, as their rage mounts fast and can occur with little or no provocation. When a rage episode appears unavoidable, managing the moment is the order of the day and it is important to invoke just the right level of intervention. Safety is paramount—safety of the child, their classmates, as well as oneself. This likely means that you will need to physically intercede and perhaps restrain the child to secure the safety of everyone. Rage episodes requiring physical restraint can last a long time. The child becomes engorged with adrenalin, and their stamina can seem limitless. Once the rage episode reaches its apex, a different set of skills is required. This involves a restoration of order as the child is guided back to a state of equilibrium. Self-regulation is the goal. This usually involves a gradual return of trust by relieving one restraint, then another (e.g., hands being held are released, one hand at a time), contingent upon the child displaying *settling behaviour*. Once all restraints have been removed and the child has returned to a state of self-regulation, the rebuilding process can commence. Often there are several consequences that the child must process before they can return to the classroom (e.g., restitution for damages, acts of contrition toward offended individuals, reparations for one's mess, etc.). Such resolutions need to be handled judiciously and humanely, as the child needs to return to the classroom with a certain amount of dignity. It's more of a negotiation than an arbitrary doling out of consequences. The reason for this is that the child needs to feel some level of control over their situation. The acceptance of blame and expressions of contrition need to be coached as pre-conditions for re-entry into social groups.

Returning to Calvin. Please allow me to indulge myself in the psychodynamics of Calvin's case, but I will reiterate that I am not a psychologist. My views however, come from countless exchanges with Calvin and his family as well as the mental health professionals that helped me with Calvin, so I feel entitled to opine on the origins of his rage. Calvin's rage appeared to come from his deep need to control. He had to dominate, and I suspect this may have originated from observing his overbearing father in an alcohol-induced moment. Did viewing his mother submitting to the abuse reigning down on her set the seed for Calvin's need to dominate? I was taught that children like Calvin are constantly testing the strength of those attempting to manage them. They want the affirmation that someone worthy is in control of them.

If you abate, you are deemed untrustworthy, too weak to intercede on their behalf. Such children's anxiety often stems from these perceptions of weakness. It may not appear as such at the time, but they really want you to prevail over them so they can feel secure. I found this paradox to be mostly true for the many troubled youngsters I encountered in my practice but less so with Calvin. There was something deeper going on with him, something out of reach of conventional thinking. I suspected a psychosis.

He was a stocky kid, with a strong athletic build. He was always on the hunt for something to exploit, be it a classmate or a school rule. When he sensed weakness, he would pounce on it. At his best, he could be congenial and eerily pleasant to deal with, but one was always wary of letting one's guard down. He would do "evil things" that made you suspicious about the prevalence of a deeper disturbance, a hole in his soul perhaps. Here is a particularly repugnant example. One day, he uncharacteristically offered Kenny, a classmate of his, some jellybeans. Kenny hesitated, rightfully so, as he had incurred bullying from Calvin in the past and was leery of Calvin's sudden generosity. But the jellybeans proved to be too tempting for Kenny and he eventually accepted them. While munching them down, Calvin immediately erupted into the most hideous laughter, confusing Kenny and everyone else in the room. Calvin, between overt belly-jiggles of laughter, boldly confessed to sticking them in his rectum before offering them to Kenny. This may or may not have been true, but the fact he contrived this ruse highlights the pathology behind his motives. In Calvin's mind, Kenny was weak, and weakness was abhorrent to him. He had to dominate. Retracing the psychological breadcrumbs that led to this, it may be reasonable to postulate he detested his mother's "weakness". She herself was a meek and mild individual who had endured abuse at the hands of her husband's alcohol-induced rages. She seemed unable to break the cycle of abuse and stayed by her husband's side. Calvin may have seen how perilous this was for his mother and despised her for allowing herself to be victimized that way. Again, this is only conjecture on my part, but Calvin's predilection for violence can not be disputed. Many times, I and those who were assisting me would have to physically restrain him through violent rages for the safety of everyone in the room. One time, he even attacked me with a baseball bat. These rages could last for hours rendering everyone, including Calvin, totally exhausted. In the end, he would make commitments to seek other means to deal with his frustrations, but time and time again these commitments would be broken, and he would resort back to physical intimidation. At one point, the Superintendent in our school district provided a one-on-one behavioural counsellor to shadow Calvin throughout the day so that I could concentrate on my primary role of teaching. This expert's involvement was helpful, but it was not the end of Calvin's rages. They persisted until he was eventually admitted to a treatment centre.

I had Calvin in my ED class for two years prior to his placement at the treatment centre. There were many positive interactions I had with him over those years, and I want to guard against stripping this young man of his self-worth. He should not be defined solely by his rage. He was quite athletic, and I tried to capitalize on that by taking an interest in his hockey and soccer pursuits. I attended a few of his games. I encouraged him to try out for our school basketball team where I was the coach. I even included him in a Christmas skit I was arranging for the school (he could be a bit of a ham at times), thinking that the influence of the non-ED students would be beneficial for him. Also, I was running a lot at the time, and I encouraged him to participate in an upcoming 10K race I had entered. I felt the non-combative nature of running might become an appropriate, stress-reducing alternative. His discipline in preparing for the event was praiseworthy. He ran the entire distance with me and seemed genuinely proud of his accomplishment. I believe these activities were mostly beneficial for him, but it wouldn't take much for him to unravel. An errant clip from extra-enthusiastic opponent or a verbal jab about how he was performing, would launch him into a rage episode, leaving one to wonder if he would ever conquer the demons that possessed him.

After he was moved to the treatment centre, I lost track of his progress. Things must have improved, as he eventually ended up in a high school where a friend of mine taught. I found out that he managed to complete his high schooling, not without a few altercations, but he finally graduated. His participation in sports was reported to be the key. If he were suspended from school, he would be prevented from playing football and hockey, two sports he enjoyed and excelled at. My friend suggested he may have been given a few "gifts" in order to complete the academic requirements. This did not surprise me, as Calvin could charm his way out of most things.

At the beginning of this chapter, I mentioned bumping into Calvin's father one day, quite by accident. Calvin would have been in his 20s at the time. His father and I chatted a bit. He seemed well and, from his demeanour, I suspected he had turned a corner on his addiction to alcohol. When the topic changed to Calvin, he winced and told me of his conviction for a robbery he had committed and his subsequent incarceration. His father claimed that drugs were the problem. Drugs may have been a symptom, but they weren't the primary cause of his problems. That much I knew.

I'll end with this. I mentioned stumbling upon Calvin's obituary while preparing for this chapter. The funeral home's announcement identified Calvin's parents and his two brothers as mourning the loss of their son and brother. The narrative was brief and may have been written by the funeral home. It had that institutional feel to it. Interestingly, the obituary included his high school graduation picture. Here, at his funeral, was this singular memory of an accomplishment that had occurred some thirty years prior. It must have been a moment of great pride for his aging parents, perhaps their only one. Had nothing memorable happened in those intervening years? Sad. There was also a place for comments from others who knew him. There were only two. One was from a woman who expressed her condolences to Calvin's parents and the other was from a former friend of Calvin's. I read the one from his friend several times. It was written as a letter to Calvin as if he were still alive. He called him "Bro". It was wildly inappropriate, commenting about the time they both got drunk and passed out. The writer alluded to a wrestling match that ensued in the middle of this drunken foray, claiming Calvin had pinned him to the floor, and adding it was the only time in his life he had ever been pinned. I'm sure the author of this note intended it as a gesture of respect. This incident appeared to have occurred sometime after Calvin had been released from prison, as there was a reference to their friendship experiencing a long absence. The point here is, there were only two contributions to this obituary page: one stolid expression of sympathy for the family and the other, a testimony to a continuation of a very unsettled life. The absence of comments spoke louder than the two posted. Calvin had indeed died suddenly, and unfortunately, to no one's surprise.

As I penned this last sentence, I felt great remorse. I think of the enormous number of resources that were directed toward helping Calvin conquer his demons and for what end? The futility of it all. Where does this leave me? How can I attach a sense of pride to his life, one of continual disappointment? Well, of course I can't. Over the years, I encountered a few students like Calvin, perhaps not quite as severe. Not all, of course, but with similar disappointing outcomes. How can this not lead to despair? I've wondered about this quite often. I think of it this way. My role, as I saw it, was to light candles in dark rooms. Some were big and some were small. With time, some flickered and died while others burned on. My task, it would seem, was not to keep every corner of the room awash in light, but rather to provide enough illumination for students like Calvin to find some unlit ones in the shadows. Ones that can be lit from the flame of the others. For some, there doesn't seem to be sufficient light for them to do that, and they remain in perpetual darkness.

Chapter 8: Liar, Liar, Pants on Fire

She was just a wisp of a woman, smaller than I expected. She had a thick accent, possibly Scandinavian. I don't remember her name. I'll call her Renata. "Is Rosario around by any chance?" My question to her probably spilled out nonchalantly, as I was certain her answer would confirm my suspicion. Her answer? Well, let's just say that it left me with a profound sense of shame that lingers some 30 years later. "He's out with the dogs," was her reply. There it was. I had wanted to catch Rosario in the lie. And, for what end, I am not sure. I suppose I wanted the truth to set him free, some misdirected aphorism like that. But he was indeed telling the truth all along. Shame on me for doubting him.

Rosario was a student in a special program I headed up at a local high school. My role was to work with students who were delinquent in one form or another, and my task was to get them on track before they became dropouts. A few of these students also had learning disabilities. Typically, they were in grades nine or ten. Their files were thick with accounts of failed interventions. The approach I used involved tapping into their interests in the hope of finding an academic connection to some of their course work. I enjoyed complete freedom in this role, as my program was considered the last resort for these wayward students. Rosario was habitually truant and way behind in his assignments. When he was at school, he would get into squabbles with his peers which resulted in a string of incident reports, detentions, and even suspensions. Usually, these squabbles originated from stories he would invent, wild concoctions that provoked insinuations of lying. His lies were typically about outlandish things—supermodels as girlfriends, being the leader of a gang, or getting a speeding ticket for driving his motorcycle three times the legal speed limit. He was only 14! His peers would challenge him on his stories, and fights would inevitably ensue. What made it worse—he would never back down from a story, never confessing it to be untrue. I felt his habitual lying was an obstacle that needed to be addressed.

One day, I may have been exploring possible career paths for him to consider. I probably asked him where he saw himself employed in five- or ten-years' time. His answer gave me a jolt. "I want to win the Iditarod." That's right, the world-famous dog race held in Alaska every year from Anchorage to Nome. It can last for over two gruelling weeks. Not only do competitors need expertise in handling unruly sled dogs, but they also need to know how to survive in some of the most inhospitable territory in the world. His answer would have been preposterous from most anyone's perspective, but when you considered Rosario lived in a metropolitan area in Southern Ontario where comparatively mild winters were the norm, his response to my question seemed detached from reality. At the time, I may have thought lining up the impediments to his outlandish goal might nudge him toward reason. I asked him to tell me more about his goal. His story was a compelling one and contained details that drew me in. He claimed he had a friend (Renata) who raised and trained sled dogs. She lived in an old farmhouse on the edge of town. *She? A farmhouse?* My suspicions were aroused. Then he told me more. He described her as an older lady, a widow who needed help running her operation. This story was really getting fantastical! He provided vague directions to Renata's place, but they contained enough specificity for me to think there was a kernel of truth to what he was telling me. Something like, "The farmhouse was white, back from the road, hidden by bushes, just over the train tracks off Huron Road". He said he went there almost every day after school. I let him think I bought it. I decided to sleuth a bit and pay him a surprise visit. I was certain his story wouldn't pan out. Then I'd confront him. He'd have to admit to lying. Facing the truth would somehow benefit him. That must have been how I thought about it. So, I went and tracked this Renata person down.

Shortly after Renata confirmed she not only knew Rosario but that he was also involved with her dogs, I heard some barking off in the distance. She pointed to a trail that went alongside her barn. There was a decommissioned rail line that meandered off into the countryside. The barking became louder as I looked on. Within no time at all, Rosario appeared, expertly leading a team of about six energetic dogs pulling a motorless All Terrain Vehicle (it was early fall or late spring, so no snow). For the next half hour or so I stood to the side while I watched Rosario bring order to the chaos involved in untethering his energetic charges, storing their traces, giving them water, and returning them to their kennels. I chatted with Renata while I waited for him to finish. I learned she was indeed a widow, and she confessed to depending on Rosario very much. She was older and probably found the physical part of managing the dogs more taxing than it once was. She explained how she happened to catch Rosario in with her dogs one day. He had trespassed and snuck into an exercise run. She was surprised her dogs took to him so easily. A relationship ensued soon after that.

In addition to breeding sled dogs, she also bred a kind of blue-eyed collie. I mention this subsequently, as I recall also becoming acquainted with Rosario's knowledge of genetics, knowledge he picked up from working with Renata. Still fresh in my mind was the jaw-dropping discussion I had with him as he showed me the collies, explaining how dominant and recessive genes are expressed in the dogs' eye colour. This was a kid who couldn't (or wouldn't) pass grade ten science? Rosario's story was an astonishing one, one that strained credulity.

So, let me summarize. Rosario, on the surface, had very little going for him. He wasn't doing well in school, and all the signs indicated that it was a place where he didn't want to be and, I am sure, he felt it was also a place where no one seem to want him. Somehow, he bumped into this eccentric widow who saw something in him that no one else was able to see. Together, a bond flourished. The rest, as they say, is history. The best of human nature spawned a relationship where trust and mutual respect was able to flourish unimpeded by what may have been projected on him by the school system. Everything I had hoped to accomplish with him in my program was happening on its own, completely without my intervention. He was able to initiate and sustain a positive social bond with an unusual, but seemingly well-intended person. He not only worked hard, without compensation, but he also equipped himself with the essential skills and knowledge that might lead him to his goal, a goal unattainable to most including me. When I think of this and ponder how inadequate my own career-nurturing choices were at Rosario's age, I am ashamed.

Doubt can be a pernicious thing. White lies, even exaggerated boasts, can survive unchallenged in the social world. But when untruths cross over and become blatantly improbable, they are usually confronted with doubt. Doubt then becomes the antidote for lying, arresting its proliferation on the spot. When it doesn't, the lying is a problem. And, so it was with Rosario. He was surrounded with others' doubts most days, but he kept his dream private—the one that was attached to a surprising reality. I thought it odd he didn't boast about it. Why? I couldn't figure it out. I have pondered this over the years and have analyzed it this way. Rosario may have been inventing his fantastic lies, not to gain friends, but to keep his peers at arm's-length. He could safely reside as an outcast, his wild concoctions becoming a smokescreen, hiding his true life from their persistent disparagement. His life with Renata and her dogs was the part of his life he cared about the most. They say, the best place to hide a leaf is in a forest. His Iditarod fantasy was his leaf. To the best of my knowledge, he never disclosed to his peers his interest in the Iditarod nor his arrangement with Renata. That remained his precious secret, a tiny truth hidden amongst the whoppers he blatantly told every day. Who would believe it even if the truth leaked out? After all, he lied about everything else.

When I happened upon him and Renata that day, I had the feeling he knew my true motives. I was there impersonating someone who was supposedly enthused about his student's curious ambition. Of course, this was not true. I was there to disclose his lie, and worse, I perpetrated the guise of shamelessly feeding an image I may have had of myself as an arbiter of the truth. As I think about the phrase, *you're a liar*, an oft heard remark from one of Rosario's peers, and compare it to me tacitly thinking him a liar all the while, falsely projecting a sincere belief in his story, I find I had been more of the liar than he. I represented a school system, a system that sanctioned success, and here I was doubting his aspirations, covertly yes, but it was still doubt. My institutional role, unlike that of his peers, made my suspicions more pernicious, lurking in the weeds, hobbling ambition by setting "truth traps". I doubted Rosario until I didn't, and that is the only truth that survived that day. I wish I could take that moment back, the one where he first told me of his interest in the Iditarod. I have since learned that the resilience of any one's dream to withstand the headwinds of time is best discovered through the wear and tear of one's own experience, and not from the lecturing tone of another's doubt, especially a teacher's.

Let me return to the structure of this memoir. Is Rosario's story one of *villain*, *victim*, or the *vanquished*? Certainly, my initial motive was propelled by a perception of him being a kind of *villain* with his persistent lying. Had I thought more of him as a *victim*, a young man whose sense of alienation and anomie, affecting him so profoundly that he had to invent outlandish things to survive, I may have handled things differently. For example, instead of trying to discredit him, suppose I accepted his story uncontested and met with his English teacher to propose an alternative assignment for Rosario. An essay on the Iditarod, legitimizing his interest in sled dog racing and providing him with an avenue toward better grades? Or met with his Science teacher, and proposed a project on dominant and recessive gene expression in the eye colour of collie dogs? Maybe, I should have embraced his interest in dogs and connected him with a veterinarian? Wouldn't these approaches erase some of the negative perceptions teachers (and others) held about him? I suppose there is always the possibility that he could have been lying about the sled dogs, but what would it have cost me to believe his story right off the bat? Would it have been detrimental to him to leave his lie unchallenged? I'm still not sure if there would have been a better path forward. The point here is that perceptions of *villain* or *victim* alter one's approach, and Special Educators must be mindful of this every day.

I also must consider *vanquishment* in understanding Rosario. In school, he behaved like a defeated kid, operating as if school held no promise for him—an illegitimate student if you will, a "bastard" of the stubborn traditions of an inflexible school system. The curriculum held no relevance for him, and the lofty goals of better grades and post-secondary study were woefully out of reach for this young man. They were for other kids. Not him. When there is nothing to gain, there is also nothing to lose. This is an unfortunate by-product of making square pegs fit into round holes like the school system is wont to do.

Rosario's other lies persisted long after my visit with him and Renata. His academic growth continued to fall precipitously. Whatever my program was trying to accomplish with him, it wasn't working. He may have continued one more year, but eventually he dropped out of high school all together. I lost track of him. On a few occasions, I have read news results from the current year's Iditarod and the progress its competitors have made. I look for his name, but I have never found it. A few years ago, I returned to the town where I was teaching Rosario after a long absence. I happened to be in the vicinity of Renata's old farm. It was no longer there. In its place was a small cluster of sprawling estate homes, completely erasing any sign of her dog breeding operation. Interestingly, the abandoned train track was still there, only it had been converted into a pleasant hiking/biking trail complete with a paved pathway and a small post holding a dispenser of dog-poop bags, just about where Renata's barn gate would have been, the spot where Rosario would begin his training run with the dogs every day after school. I smiled at the thought. A curious irony, don't you think?

Chapter 9: It's Not What It Looks Like

Vanquishment, the perception of what the person lacks as opposed to what the person possesses, can be insidious. This is especially true when dealing with children with physical manifestations of their disability. Such perceptions seep in undetected, often seeding doubts about a child's competence. Consider when meeting a youngster in a wheelchair struggling with the symptoms of cerebral palsy, twisted in torment as they grunt out approximations of their intent; or, when greeting a child with Down syndrome with their characteristic facial features; and even when viewing a child with a simple ocular misalignment such as strabismus (crossed eyes). All these can generate misappropriated assumptions about restricted competence. We instantly define them in terms of their disability rather than viewing them as people who are abled in some other way. Think of Stephen Hawking, the famous scientist. If he had been living at a time when the technological enhancements necessary for him to communicate were not yet invented, one's view of his enormous intellect would be severely restricted. Consider the inadequate attributions one might render viewing him, squished uncomfortably into a chair, his head bent in despair with no way of communicating, his brilliance churning away in that head of his, quite out of view from those that might benefit from his genius. Vanquishment works this way, perhaps less obviously, but it can extract a piece of one's humanity.

I have learned that there are subtleties to these kinds of biases that snag like tuffs of cotton on Velcro. It surfaces in how we talk to these folks, unintentionally devaluing fragments of their humanness as we dumb down our language and back off our expectations. The anecdotes I will be providing in this chapter attempt to illustrate how some individuals are able to see beyond the optics. Before I commence though, I must confess to presenting these cases with their disability in full view, and in the same breath, unabashedly caution readers against such practices. I apologize in advance for this obvious hypocrisy, but I feel by acknowledging it up front, I have absolved myself from at least some blame. Please forgive me.

I'll start with Kent. Kent may have been 14 when I first had him as a student. He remained a student of mine throughout his full high school program, so my knowledge of him and his challenges is extensive. Kent's life started out like most any other young boy's. He was bright, curious, and his mind raced from one impulse to another. "Full of mischief." It was the way his older brother described him when he came to pick him up one day after school. At age 7, everything stopped for Kent, as well as for his entire family. It was a car accident. The gear shift of his father's car penetrated Kent's right eye and plunged into his brain that fateful day. Kent's seatbelt was unhooked when the car struck and he was thrust violently on to the centre console. In addition to losing his eye, there was significant brain damage to his limbic system, the emotional centre of the brain. The right side of Kent's face needed to be reconstructed and he was fitted with a prosthetic eye. It took countless number of surgeries to get him to the point where I began my relationship with him as a student in my charge, some seven years later.

One can easily imagine how grotesque the right side of his face looked, especially after the facial reconstruction, but if you saw him from the back or from the left side, he wouldn't look any different from any other young teenager. He could still walk, jump, and even run. His speech was completely unaffected by the accident. If pushed, he could read and write, albeit below his age level, but certainly he could accomplish this with close to full understanding of what he was reading or writing. Mathematics was a bit more troubling for him. Socially, I would describe him as chatty and congenial to everyone he met—his mood never seemed to change. He was always oddly cheery. So, what was the problem? The trauma to his limbic circuitry rendered it unable to function as it should. He had no discernable emotion. So, instead of an emotional range typical of a teenage boy—think happy, sad, angry, proud, even scared—he had only cheery. Just cheery all the time. Not too bad so far, right? Well, it was bad. In fact, it was horrible, and it was this emotional stasis that defined his disability, one that would severely limit him for the remainder of his life. It not only affected him but those around him.

I spent most of my teaching career working with students who had difficulty regulating their emotions. I have introduced a few of them in this memoir. For many of them, achieving a level of calm like Kent's would have been an enormous achievement. However, having no emotional range whatsoever was a completely different kind of disabling condition. My interaction with Kent revealed this. I'll start at the beginning.

It may have been the first week of high school for Kent. In preparation for receiving him in my class, I had read his file and spoke to his mother (his parents divorced after the accident). I was told what to expect. I felt informed. As it turned out, I was wrong. Very wrong. The school district where I worked was big on inclusive environments for students with disabilities and I did my best to ensure this for Kent. I had him enrolled in a gym class where he could interact with youngsters his own age. I met with the Physical Education teacher and gave him pertinent background information and described what Kent might be able to do and not do. Initially, I walked him to PE class, got him comfortable with the change routine, and made sure he was settled. For the first few days, it seemed like this was a good fit for him. He was not athletic, but he could reasonably participate in most of the activities. His gym teacher assigned a few well-adjusted students the task of including Kent in what they were doing. I gradually withdrew my support to let the benefits of normalization take root. A few days later, I received a call from his mother. "Where is Kent?" was her question. "He's in gym class" was my response. "No, he isn't," was her rebuttal. "He's at the police station!" she added, not trying to conceal her anger. It turns out that gym was outside that day and Kent wandered off unnoticed as the group spread out over the field. While the class was occupied madly kicking balls around imagined opponents, Kent slipped into a nearby convenience store and helped himself to some candy. The store manager called the police. This was my introduction to what it is like to live in a brain that does not know what guilt or shame feels like. He simply couldn't feel these things because his limbic system was not functioning correctly. Hence, shoplifting was no more than going to the cupboard for a snack. Whether he had a right to that particular cupboard or not, wasn't processed by him. You could explain to him what he did was wrong, but he wouldn't get it. He wasn't being devious. The ethical barrier that restricts most of us when contemplating taking what does not belong to us was non-existent for him. He would do it again...and again...each time with a similar outcome.

I learned food was a compulsion for him. However, hunger was not the driving force here. I suspect the hook for him was more the pleasurable sensation of tasting sweet or fatty foods. You might think he would have a weight problem with this type of condition, but he was as trim as could be, most likely because this obsessive behaviour was well-managed. His mother, out of necessity, adopted a militaristic approach to food. She had a lock on the refrigerator and any cupboard that contained food. She did not send him to school with a lunch either. Instead, Kent had a pre-arranged punch card for use in the cafeteria that specified what he could purchase for lunch. He had to sit with a supervisor to keep him from eating discarded food from other student's trays, or from going through the trash bin for waste, or even worse, scraping gum off the underside of cafeteria tables. Scrutiny over food access was an essential part of schooling him. Scolding him or punishing him for this type of thing had no enduring effect beyond the immediate moment. Once there was no one there to redirect his obsession, he would follow his compulsion to the nearest food source.

One might think social pressure could moderate his lack of restraint. Imagine the scorn heaped upon him when his teenage peers saw him under a cafeteria table looking for discarded gum or his head buried in a trash bin feasting on a half-eaten tray of french fries. I intercepted Kent entertaining a small group of boys at a cafeteria table one day. Unable to restrain their cruel curiosities, they mercilessly goaded him into taking out his prosthetic eye—to which he complied quite enthusiastically, I might add—mistaking their collective repulse for good fun. He was not able to process their belligerent gagging as ridicule. I won't elaborate on my reaction to this group. Let's just say it didn't happen again.

An unfortunate, but revealing incident occurred one day. Kent was enrolled in an Industrial Arts (IA) class. As I remember it, his IA teacher was delayed getting to class and some boisterousness, typical of that age group, ensued while they waited. It involved punching each other's shoulder in an apparent demonstration of machoism to see how much pain one could endure. This was not fighting, merely horseplay amongst boys in 9th or 10th grade, an age where immaturity erupts quite spontaneously. Kent must have thought this to be intriguing and he invited one of the other students to punch him in the shoulder. The boy obliged, breaking Kent's collar bone in the process. Kent's response was interesting. He did not get angry with the student. He did not cry out. He felt pain, enormous pain, but not anger. He got up and left, his shoulder listing to the side. When he returned to my classroom, I could see something was wrong with him wincing in pain, quite different from his usual cheeriness. He revealed what happened in the most matter-of-fact way. "Isaac punched me. My arm is sore." One could easily imagine this was not a small problem for the school, nor for me, but it was telling of how vulnerable this young man was. Kent was in a sling for several weeks, and his collar bone healed eventually. His recollection of the moment was clear for him, but he did not project blame or resentment on the offending student. As part of Isaac's reconciliation, he was to confront Kent and apologize for hurting him. Isaac (who had no reputation for violence), was deeply concerned about what he had done and wanted to make it right. Kent's response to this very sincere apology? He shouted, "Give me five, man!" Not, "Thanks for your apology," or "What you did really hurt, don't do it again". Nothing but, "Give me five, man!" The social elixir of a sincere apology, the key ingredient to reconciliation, went completely over his head. He couldn't comprehend that his classmate was seeking his forgiveness, a condition quite foreign to Kent.

Learning is most robust when it occurs in combination with the full application of one's personal resources and the learner's emotional attachment to the outcome of the task being learned. This is called intrinsic motivation. I had Kent as a student long enough to recognize that his cognitive development was stuck at the same level it was prior to the accident, and he functioned as if no learning had taken place during the intervening time that had elapsed since the accident. I will admit to boldly trespassing on the field of neuroscience when reporting that Kent's damage to his limbic system left him shrouded in a blanket of pervasive apathy that thwarted any kind of meaningful learning. My best guess is he simply could not feel the intrinsic gush of contentment in conquering a challenge or feeling proud of a visible accomplishment, even though he was capable. Nothing. He would initially begin a task, but within minutes his dedication to the task would languish and he would while-away the time looking about the room hoping to bump into something more compelling. One-on-one monitoring yielded no appreciable benefit. Judicious praise couldn't launch him much past the starting point on any particular project either. It was the same with tangible tasks (i.e., drawing, painting, industrial arts projects) as it was with pencil and paper academics. Intrinsic satisfaction was not something he experienced. This was not the same kind of apathy seen with boredom. With boredom, students will often have their focus shift to other sources of stimulation. They may daydream or fiddle with an object. This was not the case with Kent. I never observed him in a trance-like state as one might expect with daydreaming. And, he didn't have other interests (e.g., games or toys) to syphon off his attention either. His locker was empty, save his clothing. Other than food, wandering the room for chance encounters with other students was the only source of stimulation for him. This made academic learning irrevocably stagnant.

I developed this view of him over a period of several years. Initially, I rebelled against the notion that Kent could not learn academic subjects. It went against my insistence that all children can learn, at least on some level. I recall being tacitly at odds with Kent's mother on this issue. I found her custodial approach to raising her son to be objectionable. I felt she may have given up on him—perceived him as *vanquished*. Later though, my respect for her position on Kent's needs moderated. She had learned what I was learning, long before he entered my classroom. She had to live with a severely disabled young man day and night, and I, only a few hours of the day.

At the end of Kent's fourth year of high school, I attended his graduation. I cheered along with his mother and brother as he walked across the stage, donned with cap and gown, there like all the other students to collect their diploma. The path across the stage was from right to left (not by design), thereby concealing his disfigurement from the audience. As he shook the principal's hand and accepted his diploma, he was for the moment, indistinguishable from any other student. To those in the audience who did not know him, his diploma represented all the attributes of a successful student, until he turned to face them head-on. Then, their reflexive aversion would kick in, snapping them back, aspersions of doubt seeping in, their expectations becoming calcified and guarded. With me, the one in the audience who knew him well, his diploma was not much more than a token acknowledgement of his participation in normalization. I knew nothing close to measurable academic growth occurred in this young man's past four years. I say this without any intention of disparagement. The stark reality of his condition could lead to no other conclusion. This saddened me of course, but it was something I learned to accept. To his mother, and perhaps his older brother, the graduation meant something far different—a formal acknowledgement of a life that had once flourished until it flickered out following the accident. I guess they were there to remember who he once was and not who he was to become. They had harboured no misgivings about educational transformation. They didn't expect his diploma would get him a job, nor entry into a post-secondary program. They were there to celebrate an interrupted life, one that began with considerable promise, but one that had been paused...sadly forever. They knew Kent in his pre-vanquished state, and this is how they preferred to think of him. Who could argue differently?

Next would be Brian. Goldenhar syndrome is a rare genetic disorder that usually results in dramatic disfigurement to the face. Many individuals with Goldenhar syndrome have only one working ear and only one seeing eye, although distorted vestiges of either can remain. Brian was a student who was born with this disorder. Craters where the missing ear would have been, and a dormant eye pushed up toward his temple, cast an arresting image. The image yielded an obvious uncomfortableness in those who were not in regular contact with him. He was in the Special Education program at the high school where I was teaching.

Brian had no speech. He had a few basic signs for things he wanted to communicate and a few primitive gestures he added to his repertoire. When he wanted something, he would extend his hand toward the object and wiggle his fingers while grunting enthusiastically. "Do you want this, Brian?" would result in a vigorous nod of his head and something that sounded like *hum*. Brian was a bit naughty. He could understand oral directions but wasn't always compliant. Also, he had some peculiarities that challenged one's definition of appropriateness.

One was heights. If he went missing, he could usually be found in the stairwell on the top floor, peering down the gap between floors. That particular vantage point would excite him endlessly. He would shout with glee, dropping things through the gap and then racing down the stairs to retrieve them. Once engaged in this practice, it was difficult to get him to cease. Plastic film, the type used with overhead projectors, was another fetish for him. He would rub the film on parts of his body or place it on the floor and lie on it. This appeared to be sexual in nature stretching one's notion of acceptable behaviour.

One person in the Special Education Department at the high school where Brian attended was very effective with him, and it wasn't me. Mary was a teaching assistant that worked with him. She wasn't particularly good with any other student, but she was good with him. She and Brian seem to have a special bond. The Department operated in a large open space where small groups could convene without interfering with each other. On a few occasions, probably when Mary was away, I would be more directly involved with Brian than I would ordinarily. During those times, I became acutely aware of Mary's extraordinary skill in dealing with him. She could accomplish things I could not. He simply would not comply to my requests, despite my best effort. To be frank, I was not particularly fond of Mary, nor she of me for that matter, but I had to acknowledge her ability with Brian. She had these moments where the two of them would have a type of normalized interaction which was mystifying. She would say a few things. He would gesticulate, grunt, and groan and somehow get his message across to her. The communication seemed to mimic real communication, meaningful exchanges. She could not only get him to do things but could also redirect him, getting him to desist doing things he shouldn't. Curiously, she wasn't particularly gentle with him. She would scold him like an angry parent might. He always seemed to respond to her. If I used a similar tone with him, it would erupt in a temper tantrum that was often violent. He was a big strong boy. This was something I wanted to avoid. I was envious of her mastery over him, but despite my best efforts, I could not replicate her effectiveness.

I'll end this chapter with one final example. Scott was a young man in my homeroom at a high school I was working at. Scott had multiple diagnoses. He had been in a wheelchair since infancy. He was severely palsied with uncontrollable muscle spasms that twisted him into crippling contortions. He had seizure-like tremors where he would scream violently while jamming his fist into his mouth and biting furiously until it bled. Life seemed to be an unending torment for him. He had no discernable language, neither receptive nor expressive. There would be no cognitive scale that could validly represent his ability to learn even the most fundamental of tasks. He needed 24-hour care. His family were devoted to his needs but they felt, rightly or wrongly, institutional care to be too restrictive for him (and them). Having him be with typically developing children provided an intangible benefit that only they could feel. I bumped into his mother one day in the grocery store, quite by accident. We made small talk for a bit and then she gave me a complement. She told me Scott really enjoyed my homeroom. It was difficult for me to comprehend her comment. *Was she just being gracious? How would she know if her son enjoyed anything?* These were thoughts that raced through my mind, thoughts that remained unvoiced. She would have had to infer this somehow. Scott at the time was approaching 20. She had fed him, changed his diapers, consoled him through thousands of raging torments for two decades. I, on the other hand, saw him for 15 minutes a day in homeroom. She was able to pick up on some subtle manifestation of contentment that she felt was noteworthy. No one would know this but her. So, what would have been different in our homeroom environment that Scott could derive some level of contentment from in those brief 15 minutes? All I could think of was the introduction of a beachball. Homeroom was routine in every way—the national anthem, the morning prayer and then announcements. Homeroom was scheduled for 15 minutes regardless of how long it took to accomplish all these tasks. There was usually 5 minutes of flex time tagged on to the end. With teenagers, stagnant time can be a problem, so filling those last five minutes seemed essential. I brought in a giant beachball for us to volley back and forth while we waited for the bell to ring. The beachball was a hit (excuse the pun). Occasionally, the ball would land on Scott and he would shudder. It appeared kinaesthetically pleasurable to him. The kids noticed and began to gently launch the ball towards Scott. Their excitement was palpable. Since his mother was never present for our homeroom, I can only assume Scott conveyed a tiny piece of new contentment to her, a piece only she could discern.

* * *

Let me wrap this up. Inclusive school environments such as the one Kent, Brian, and Scott experienced, create opportunities for normalization. Some readers may not be aware that children with such unique needs are purposely placed in amongst children without disabilities as much as is appropriate to achieve this normalization. The meaning of what is "appropriate" has been argued about since the 1970s. What benefit do children, both typically-developed and non-typical ones, derive from such a practice? How much is appropriate? There are lots of competing perspectives on this and none yield answers that don't involve compromise for educating either type (see Chapter 11). Thoughts such as, *How can I relate to this person?* or even, *Should I relate to this person?* might percolate below the surface as mainstreamed students begin to have regular contact with severely disabled ones. This of course happens with regularity, but relating to these students in meaningful ways, well that is another question. The point here is, someone in the cases shared above could relate to these individuals, enabling reciprocal exchanges in one form or another. This might be out of reach for typical onlookers, but it doesn't mean that the relationships weren't genuine. They are able to see beyond the *vanquishment*. I will expand on this notion in a subsequent chapter (see Chapter 12).

Chapter 10: Family

"I might not be here for a couple of days. My mom and dad are coming to get me." I remember this statement like it was yesterday although it has been almost 30 years since I heard Timmy announce their arrival to his classmates. Timmy was a "lifer", a term we gave to children who were wards of the province for most of their childhood. They were usually deemed unadoptable if their mental health had not improved sufficiently by ages 9 or 10. I can't recall the specifics, but Timmy came into care as a toddler, first in a series of foster homes and eventually in the residential treatment facility where I served as one of his teachers. He would have been about ten years old when he made this announcement about his parents coming to get him. It was a remarkable statement for a lot of different reasons.

Timmy was very bright but incalculably damaged by something in his past. It may have been abuse, neglect, or abandonment. It may have been all three. The point here is that he was a disturbed young man, and the likelihood of him successfully transitioning into the less restrictive environment of an adoption was remote. He had enormous difficulty with healthy social interactions. He fractured relationships at the slightest provocation. He could be cunning and pathologically manipulative, turning the charm on and off like a tap. In short, there were not only red flags but stop signs. He was amongst the most troubled youngsters I would ever encounter. So, the announcement on that day was a surprise. Unbeknown to me, a childless couple was seeking to adopt, and their application had proceeded to the point where they were considering Timmy as a possibility. Why him? I was never really sure, but it made me wonder about the judiciousness of this decision, theirs as well as the adoption agency's. When Timmy made this announcement, the process was very preliminary. Apparently, an initial informal meeting was suggested, and Timmy was made privy to the possibility he might be meeting someone new. He naïvely concluded (or wished) this was a done deal and he was being adopted. He would have a mom and dad just like most of his fellow residents. He thought that's all there was to it—the entire carnage of his life instantly washed away in a kind of Cinderella moment. Well, it is never that easy. Usually, the adopted child is the one who is most reticent about using the "mom" and "dad" moniker. Not for Timmy though. There was no hesitation at all, no period of adjustment, no trust-building phase. Nothing. Sadly, the adoption never progressed beyond a few exploratory get-togethers and Timmy had to endure more rejection. What is pertinent to this chapter is the tragic nature of Timmy's cry for something amorphous, the concept of a family, someone to call mom and dad. Over the years, he had seen children come in and out of care, often getting picked up by their new parents. He had wondered why no one ever came for him. The feeling of being abandoned must have burrowed deep and lingered long.

The pull of needing to belong to a family is an enormous one, and this pull does not seem to weaken even if the structure of that family is not entirely sound. Having a family, in whatever form it takes, seems to be everything for children. Timmy's story is illustrative of this. I'll share a few more examples of family structures that function at the edge of normal.

I'll provide another example. "The province could have saved a lot of money if they just bought the guy another tent." The quip was intended as a humorous one, offered by my colleague as he and I passed one of the consultation rooms where Eddy and his father were having a supervised visit with the social worker assigned to his case. There was a satirical wisdom to my colleague's comment that made me question what we were trying to do for Eddy. Eddy was seven years old when he was brought into care at the residential facility where I was working. He and his father had been camping illegally in a wooded area on the edge of town when their tent caught fire and burned to the ground. The Fire Department alerted the Police, and the Police contacted Children's

Services, and that is how Eddy ended up in our facility. Eddy and his father were vagabonds who lived incognito in surrounding rural areas, surviving by their wits, never staying in one spot long enough to bring attention to themselves. The fire brought an abrupt end to it all. Eddy was deemed a ward of the province.

Eddy had never attended school. In fact, Eddy never had any socialization with other children at all. I cannot recall the specifics, but I do recall Eddy had been reared by his father since he was a toddler. Somewhere along the way, the two of them broke from society and drifted away. The authorities were worried that something sinister may have been happening between Eddy and this man who claimed to be his father. They stepped in to "rescue" him from what appeared to be a harmful situation. As it turned out, Eddy's father had legal custody of his son and there was absolutely no indication of abuse. Other than him not attending school, nor having a permanent dwelling, Eddy seemed sufficiently cared for, albeit in primitive ways. His father had taught him some fundamental life skills appropriate enough to navigate the margins of society. More importantly, he taught him how to survive on his own without the help of others. Eddy could snare a rabbit or pluck a squirrel from a tree with his sling shot more easily than I could purchase a package of hotdogs. He knew what the best material was for lighting a fire and could get one going in an instant even in the rain. He knew how grocery stores and restaurants dispensed with their surplus food. He even knew some edible wild foods. They had perfected ways of feeding themselves without breaking the law. He was only seven! The characteristics that brought **and** kept him in residential care was his lack of socialization. He didn't know how to deal with children his own age, and he was acutely wary of adults. I don't want to understate this. Eddy's needs in this area were extreme, but I must reiterate, with the exception of the above, his father seemed to exhibit the attributes of any caring parent. Paradoxically, many of the children currently in the care of the facility where Eddy now found himself, came from parents who lacked the skills and attitude Eddy's father seemed to possess. The situation was thick with irony for all of us charged with educating this youngster, hence the aptness of my colleague's irreverent quip at the beginning of Eddy's story about the simple wisdom of purchasing a replacement tent.

Eddy remained in care for several years. He was allowed intermittent supervised visits with his father, but other than that, his upbringing from the time he was brought into care was completely administered by the province. His father was assessed to be incapable of raising this child in ways the province deemed he should. One could argue the wisdom of this now, many years later. It would seem Eddy's institutional gains did little to replace what he may have gained from his father's rearing. True, he received schooling, he was well-clothed, he was sheltered, and he never had to worry about his next meal. Most certainly, these staples are very important. But he was separated from his father against his will, and unfortunately, this separation devolved into a level of emotional carnage that put him at odds with society. As he grew older, he moved on to a facility that served adolescents. This seemed to harden him even further, and eventually he found himself in juvenile detention. After that, I lost track of him. One wonders, if someone had just bought his father another tent and sent the two of them on their way, how much better it would have been for Eddy, and perhaps for society.

One more example. Adam was a chubby little guy with a freckled face and an endearing smile. He was taken from his home for his own protection when he was about eight or nine. His parents were not abusive, but they were neglectful. I believe substance abuse was the key contributor to their difficulties rearing Adam. They were quite poor and their residence, squalid. I report this only in so far as it relates to my recollection of an event I attended with Adam that brought his current circumstances into contrast. Adam had been living in a residential facility for a year or two. His emotional and behavioural needs had stabilized, so a foster placement was arranged for Adam and he was integrated into a community school. The event I reference here is a Christmas pageant Adam participated in. His foster family could not attend, and I was asked if I could bring him home following the pageant. I consented of course (I hadn't yet met his foster parents). The directions were provided for me, and Adam and I left the school later in the evening to get him back to his foster home. The address of their home was out in the country where there were some large estate homes. I was curious about this, thinking I may have the wrong address. I remember driving up to the house on that dark, winter night to an opulent sprawl. Adam assured me we were at the right place. We were greeted by a uniformed housekeeper who cordially welcomed us in. She explained that the foster parents were at an engagement and would be returning soon. I was in shock. I left, my mind in a daze. I could not think of a more overt contrast when comparing Adam's new life with his former one. I remember quizzing him. He hated it. He couldn't explain why, just that he hated it. I asked him if they were mean, or if the opulence make him feel uncomfortable. He said they were nice to him, but he just wanted to go back home to his parents. It was as simple as that. Well, Adam did go back to his parents. It seemed to be an inauspicious move to me at the time, but it may have been me projecting my own thoughts on his circumstances. I could not assume to be the purveyor of what was right for him. I encountered Adam outside a McDonald's a few years later, and he did not look like he was doing all that well. He might have been about 14 or 15. I watched him from the window while finishing my meal. He looked slovenly and disoriented. He was talking to himself (Adam had schizophrenic tendencies). When I left the restaurant, he was gone. I never saw him again.

Adam was a loyal son, struggling with his own demons. He accepted his parents' "challenges", and regardless of how troubled they were, he had parents. That must have been all that mattered to him.

Finally, there were the twins. I worked as a clinical supervisor in an assessment clinic for a number of years. It was an interdisciplinary clinic involving psychologists, speech and language pathologists, health and well-being professionals, as well as some educators. We had an interesting case that came our way that brought into question the conventional notion of "family". An Amish community had a family who were raising twins. One of the twins (they were boys) had "twin syndrome", a condition where one fetus' access to the nutritional resources of the mother gets blocked. Subsequently, one of the twins was born under-nourished and had cognitive challenges that were consistent with that condition. The other twin was completely normal. The boys were 9 or 10 at the time they were brought in for an assessment. Our determination was that the affected twin had educational needs that could no longer be met by the educational resources supplied by the Amish community (they had their own faith-based school). What was interesting about this case was how the clinic's recommendations were processed. Firstly, it wasn't the parents that initiated the referral. It was the elders. They accompanied the family every step of the way. When we presented our assessment results and made our recommendation that the one twin receive specialized programming outside of the community (i.e., secular), it was the elders who deliberated over this decision, and not the parents. The parents' influence seemed secondary, and they were apparently quite content to abdicate their responsibility to this small group of three or four bearded men. It was good for our students (it was a teaching clinic) to experience this. It challenged their notion of family in the most dramatic way. In this instance, families were cogs in the wheel of the community. The community served its religious mission first and families were subordinate to this mission, not necessarily in the authoritarian sense, but more out of benevolence, where the family's prosperity was one with community's—a chain as strong as its weakest link perhaps. The harmony was compelling and in stark contrast to some of our other cases, where more traditional families often suffered from a surfeit of dysfunction in one form or another.

* * *

Over the years, the families of the children I served came in many shapes and sizes, each with their own strengths and limitations. Some were affluent, although most weren't. Some were two-parent families, although many were raised by a single parent, usually a mother. Some were even being raised by a grandparent. One boy in particular thought he had an older sister, but at age 10 found out she was actually his mother. Some parents adopted children with profound needs, relying on the strength of their family to assuage the many challenges their adopted son or daughter had. Some parents were doctors, lawyers, or teachers. Others were only marginally employed or unemployed. Some families had other children who also had significant problems requiring special programming, while others, only the one. And sadly, some had no parents at all. Readers will unavoidably attach their own concept of family while examining the ones I have introduced in this memoir, but they should be cautioned about casting judgement. Regardless of the rickety structure that seems to define some families, there is a curious alchemy that binds children to them. It may not look like love, attachment, or even belonging, but these relationships endure somehow—a kind of gravity anchoring them to one another despite the forces wrecked upon them. The emotional grist that binds a family survives well beyond what we think is preferential. It is a mysterious force that we would do well to acknowledge and resist the temptation to wrestle it into another form.

Chapter 11: Here Come d'Judge!

One of the most uncomfortable roles a Special Educator has is assigning grades. I'll share an incident that brings this home. About half-way through my career, I took an extra certification to teach broad field social studies at the high school level. Initially, I had no intention of using this certification, but I had to have it to qualify to teach that age group. One year, the high school where I was working needed a teacher to fill in for a course on Canadian Law at the 12th grade level. I threw my hat into the ring, thinking it might be a healthy change—a diversion from my Special Education duties for part of the day.

One particular benefit to this new venture was experiencing what it was like for a general educator to integrate students with various learning challenges (i.e., those requiring Special Education) into the regular education curriculum, especially at the high school level where course grades take on an amplified value. Of the twenty-five or so students who sat before me, perhaps half of them would be counting on the grade I assigned (as well as other grades) to graduate with sufficient scores to get them into a post-secondary program of one form or another. It was high stakes for them. In one particular section of the Canadian Law course, I had a mature student. I'll call her Lois. She was a young mother who had returned to high school to complete her diploma requirements. She would have been in her mid-twenties. She sat beside Karen. I knew Karen quite well from years prior, having had her in one of my Special Education programs at the elementary school where I once taught. Karen had cognitive challenges that restricted her capacity to learn at an age-appropriate level. Subsequently, the course expectations for her were modified. Let me assert, this was a common practice, one encouraged by the district where I worked.

As a Special Educator, I had a few strategies for this. One strategy was to reduce both the amount of content and the level of difficulty of it for Karen so that she could engage enough to feel like she belonged.

This was a private arrangement between Karen, her parents, and myself. Seems fair enough, right? Well, Lois didn't see it that way. I recall this event. I was returning a mid-term exam I had graded. I had pre-arranged some simpler questions for Karen to answer. Her answers to these would determine her final score—a score unique to Karen and Karen alone. Lois on the other hand was required to answer all the questions including the ones Karen was assigned. Since Karen and Lois sat side-by-side when the mid-term papers were being returned, Lois noticed that Karen's modified grade was either equal to hers or perhaps even a bit higher. She was deeply troubled by this apparent unfairness. She asked to speak to me out in the hall, demanding to know how it was that Karen received such a high grade when she clearly did not complete as many questions as Lois had. I was torn. Lois deserved an explanation, but Karen's integrity as a person needed to be protected as well. Lois would not be mollified by vague rebuttals referencing the need for inclusivity. She wanted to know why I seemed to be favouring Karen over her. I may have disclosed some of Karen's challenges to Lois to assuage her contempt for my apparent preferential treatment of Karen, although I thought Karen's challenges were pretty evident to most. Lois was unconvinced. She took her complaint to the Chair of the Department. It didn't go much beyond that because, as I mentioned, what I did for Karen was considered acceptable practice.

This incident reveals a lot about the difficulties in rendering important judgements about student progress when students with differing needs compete for grades in amongst the general population of students. It's competitive and students want, and deserve, fairness. But Special Education isn't fair at all. It's about making allowances for learning differences, and in honouring inclusivity, runs the risk of fouling the measuring system. Not everyone understands this, and some who do understand it, disagree with it. In the cases I have presented in previous chapters, readers might find themselves also objecting to the legitimacy of inclusive practices for at least some of these individuals.

Let me share a few more examples. As mentioned previously I was initially dually certified to teach both General Education and Special Education, K-8 level (about 20 years into my career I certified to teach High School). I had a 7th grade group for science one year. In this class, there were about three or four students who were chronic low achievers, persistently failing classroom tests and only getting by because keeping them back seemed to be an unappealing option (think *Welcome Back, Kotter*). As expected, they failed a science exam. This perpetuation of failure bothered me, and I decided to do something about it. You might say, I wanted to rescue them from this sense of *vanquishment*. I knew keeping them after school for extra tutoring was a non-starter, as it probably had been done countless times in the past. I came up with another plan. I wrote a note to their parents telling them that their son (they were all boys) had failed a science exam, and I would allow a rewrite of the exam, but only if their son would attend a series of tutorials. If they did not agree to this, their grade would stand as is. In deference to others in the class, I explained that the rewrite would be an average of their first and their second scores, ensuring that each had a shot at a passing grade but not an "A". I felt this would be viewed as fair. All the parents had to do was sign the letter indicating they either wanted their son to participate or they didn't. Well, they not only signed their support for the rewrite but added that I was to let them know immediately if their son did not show up for the study sessions. I had their unwavering support. Now here's the hard part: what do I do with these students for the week of preparing for the rewrite? I couldn't reteach a month's worth of lessons. There was too much to cover. It would be torture to cram it all into the half hour at the end of each day, for them and for me. What to do? Well, I did what any other consummate professional would do in my position. I took a shortcut. Some might even call it cheating. I distributed exact copies of the exam they had failed, and we practiced answering the questions together. Yes, practiced. They orally rehearsed the answers with me and then tried writing their responses, and I'd give them feedback until they got it right. It was very mechanistic, and I thought they'd object. They didn't. In fact, it was very effective in ameliorating their negative attitude about the topic. For them, it was like riding a two-wheeler for the first time. They couldn't believe they were doing it on their own! At the end of the week, I distributed a blank copy of the exact same exam again where they wrote their well-rehearsed answers. Unsurprisingly, their rewrite scores were much better than their first attempt. What was surprising though was the validity these youngsters placed on their revised scores. I remember one student saying to another one of his peers, "I finally beat (expletive) Derrick!" Derrick was one of the top students in the class, and this low achiever had seen Derrick get top grades every year since kindergarten while he floundered year after year. Shockingly, this student was able to dispense with years of self-disparagement in one overtly propped up moment and claim the victory over his academic adversary! His rewrite score, as contrived as it was, had washed away years of imagined subjugation. I began to wonder if I had erred. How could I put this genie back in the bottle?

I'll provide another example. I had a 13-year-old named David who was being introduced to a day-treatment program I was heading up. It was a Special Education setting for students with attention-deficit – hyperactivity disorder at a Provincial Demonstration School. He had come into the program at mid-year, so he was adjusting to his new circumstances. Initially, he was very reluctant to engage, unsure of his fit into the curriculum. One day, the taxi dropped him off early as I was putting the final touches on a geometry quiz I was preparing. He asked if I would be making him write the quiz. Working within the framework of his newness in the program, I gave him an option. After all, I didn't want him feeling *vanquished* right out of the gate. I told him that it would be up to him, but eventually I'd expect him to participate in the quiz if he wanted to pass into the next grade. He told me he didn't care about passing and had no intention of participating in the quiz. Undeterred, I continued to prepare the quiz while he watched on. I recall asking him to look at a few of the questions and tell me if he thought he could answer them. He considered each question casually, offering answers and checking with me to see if they were correct. Then class began, and I distributed the quiz. David reluctantly took a copy, projecting as much indifference as he could muster. When time was up, he handed his in announcing that he didn't try hard, and his score would mean nothing to him. As it turned out, his score was a good one, and he was quick to claim full credit for it. Clearly, I had done something for him by making his attempt at the quiz less risky by ensuring a positive result. Yet, I knew in other situations, such assurances would not be available to him, but I felt the reduction of risk would be prudent in this situation.

Grades serve many masters. I'll list them here. Firstly, they serve the students, the ones being assessed as well as the others to whom comparisons are being made (i.e., class average). Secondly, they serve the teacher as each teacher needs to know how beneficial their instruction has been. Thirdly, the parents need to know how their child is doing so they can monitor things like homework or extra tutoring. Beyond these obvious needs are systemic ones. The school, the school district, and the province or state all require grades in some form or another to observe and report trends. Grants, accreditation, teacher performance, and even jurisdictional scrutiny over curriculum depend on the statistical analysis of grades. Lastly, post-secondary institutions, employers, and scholarship-issuing bodies use grades to inform their decisions about students' readiness for higher education. That's a lot for a simple *A*, *B*, or *F* to convey even for typical students, but when grading modifications are applied to students with varying disabilities, the referential value of the grade fragments considerably.

Over the years, I have felt unsettled about the practice of grading-modification for students with disabilities. My concern is that I may have warped the definition of learning for these youngsters in my enthusiasm for sparking their re-engagement. I fear they may have left my classroom feeling falsely prepared for the real world—out the door with a fist full of Monopoly money, thinking it will buy them real stuff. Not for all, but for some, and this has bothered me. Subsequently, I have looked for justifications for such practices, examples of how humans naturally modify expectations to "even the playing field". Weekend duffers use a handicapping system so they can compete with scratch golfers more fairly. Similarly, children self-stratify games they are playing to make the teams even. They have learned that no one has fun when the scores are ridiculously unfair. A faster child gives a slower child a head start in a running race, just to make it competitive. Examples like this abound. Does anyone have to announce who the faster runner is? Or tell the golfer with the 20-handicap that their readiness for the Master's Tournament is in doubt? It seems the goal of immersive participation is a natural inclination, and not one that encourages false hope. Still, I suppose some may see these grading adjustments as counterfeit, and rightfully predict that reality will emerge as the final arbiter of my students' success. So, why do it? Aren't we just postponing the inevitable? This may be true, and I remain hard-pressed to combat such assertions. But as I think back, the prevention of *vanquishment* seems to hold as a necessary and noble motive in these contexts. *Vanquishment* is insidious. It extinguishes one's drive and promotes apathy. The grading practices identified above were intended to remove the psychological barriers that inhibit these students' efforts, and there can be no learning without effort. But effort implies risk, risk of failure. Most of us use failure as a tool to learn. *We learn by our mistakes* is the phrase. But if every mistake is catastrophic, not much learning would be done. If you jump from an airplane only to recognize you made a mistake folding your parachute, not much learning results as you plumet to the ground. Unfortunately, some of the students I had learned that risks, even mild ones, were catastrophic and needed to be avoided at all costs. Hence, my justification to chip away at feelings of *vanquishment* held by insecure learners made it safer for them to take a risk.

I also worry, although less so, of another unintended outcome of modified grading. A grade, a score, or a performance indicator of one kind or another is often used as a proxy for a complete learning profile. Assumptions are made about what this metric might represent, and these assumptions are relied upon by various downstream entities mentioned earlier. Entities such as employers, post-secondary institutions, or grant-issuing bodies may not read the footnotes explaining adjustments to the grading system. How are they to judge the scores on transcripts from a Special Education program? After all, these scores in many cases represent a significant departure from conventional scoring due to the unspecified modifications that were made for the student. Apples are not being compared to apples with many of these students. For a few of the students I have presented in this memoir, the need for such modifications will be obvious. For others though, I am less certain. I taught in a few different districts, and each had their own way of representing progress for students who experienced grading modifications. One used a coded letter, an X following the grade on the transcript that accompanied the student when they graduated. I often wondered how a $B+$ with an X beside it might be processed by a potential employer, or by post-secondary programs. Do they know what the X means? Is it possible that a student with a science score of 91% with an X beside it will get that student into pre-medicine? The possibility is a remote one for sure, but asking the question makes my point.

I am tempted to expound further on ways of evaluating students who are less typical, but I fear that would take this memoir far afield. I think readers will be well-served just knowing that summative evaluation systems for children who have unique needs have been "tampered with" and quite possibly, have become unintentionally misleading. Although addressing these shortcomings has been challenging for me, engineering systems of comparison that provide attainable goals for children, without diminishing the efforts of others, has been seen by me as a necessary part of the Special Educator's role. Renewed participation seems an honourable outcome and one I can live with even at the risk of misrepresenting the value inherent in the score. But I can not refute, it's a balancing act.

Chapter 12: It Ain't Normal

"Do you think I could do that?" was her question. Simple as it was, this question has lingered for some fifty years and it shapes my thinking on aspects of normalization to this day. It was asked of me by a 10-year-old girl as I was preparing the activities for our upcoming field day. I was teaching in a K-8 school at the time. Rita was a student in my Special Education class. She had spina bifida and was in a wheelchair. Her body was squat and compressed from the waist down. Nothing functioned as it should in her hips and legs. Everything above that point worked well. Her arms and shoulders were strong. Her hands were large and her grip firm. Cognitively she was clear-headed and assertive. She was also quite brave as this anecdote will affirm. It would have been in the late 1970s, and I am not sure of the status of what the para-culture was at that point in time. All I know is that her participation in athletics was not a consideration we had for her. Rita's seemingly innocuous question was about her competing in the activities that were being planned for that day. You know, running, jumping, throwing—not activities I felt were conducive to a person confined to a wheelchair. I confess to being a bit flummoxed. I can remember asking her how she thought it might work. She evidently had been thinking about this for quite some time. As the details started rolling out, I became increasingly uncomfortable about what she had in mind. She wanted to race but not in the way I was thinking. In my mind's eye, I saw other 10-year-old girls, all able-bodied, lining up at the starting line, with Rita alongside in her chair. *Ready-set-go* and she'd be left in their wake. She wouldn't stand a chance. She'd be humiliated. She saw it differently though. She envisioned her competitors in wheelchairs just like her! She wanted to challenge her peers to a slalom race around a series of pylons—an out-and-back kind of thing. When I raised the obvious complication of where we might find wheelchairs for this event, she simply stated she had another one at home that her mother said the school could use.

I suppose I initially expressed worry about her being hurt, but I think that might have been a smoke screen for what I was really feeling. I felt recruiting competitors might be a problem as perhaps they would be repulsed by the idea. This may have been the dominant feeling at the time. Or it may have been just me. If it was, shame on me. I'll move the story along. I must have encountered considerable headwinds with Rita's idea, but the principal agreed, and we organized the event. If no one stepped up to challenge Rita, I would get in the spare chair and give everyone a good laugh. That was my back-up plan. But on the big day, all my apprehensions were dashed. The course was laid out and the entire school gathered to watch. When I explained the event to them, I had Rita do a dry run. Then I proposed someone race her. To my astonishment, an 8th-grader stepped up. I think his name was Eddy. Of course, Eddy would be the one. He was the best athlete in the school. He was a tall, good-looking kid, and very popular. His ego was not at risk regardless of how this activity was received. Now I had a different problem. I thought Eddy might be too much for Rita. He was the captain of his hockey team, after all. As it happened, my worries were ill-founded. Rita had spent most of her life in a chair. She could maneuver that thing through stacks of teacups and not break one. And, she was strong, real strong. She completed the course in plenty of time while the rest of the school laughed at Eddy bumping into one pylon after another. It was all very good-natured of course, and Eddy shouldered the jibing well. And, if Eddy could do it, that meant it was socially safe for others, without worry of any embarrassment.

The day was a great success for Rita. She went undefeated and her status in the school catapulted to new heights. She glowed with purpose and a new sense of belonging. It was not all that remarkable when I think about it now, but it was back then. This type of integration came to be known as *reverse inclusion*. It wasn't Rita having to adapt to an able-bodied activity (i.e., inclusion), but the other way around. From what I have learned about individuals with profound disabilities since that day with Rita, *reverse inclusion* is the ultimate expression of acceptance, and those seeking to meaningfully integrate into the culture of disability should be mindful of this.

I'll provide another example of *reverse inclusion* but instead of a school-based anecdote, it is a social one. I used to swim with a gentleman who had cerebral palsy (CP). His name was Bob. Bob required a lot of support services. The disability community uses the term *involved* to describe this. Bob was quite *involved*. He lived in a supported-living facility for adults with severe disabilities. An entire floor of an apartment complex was dedicated to housing these folks. The complex encouraged independent living as much as possible, so they were housed in regular apartments complete with augmented kitchens and bathrooms. Support staff had a unit all to themselves. Bob needed a motorized chair to get around. He had one reasonably compliant arm, but the rest of his body was racked with tremors. Communicating with him was also challenging. You had to really pay attention, and even then, it took a bit of guess work. But something was always churning away in that head of his. One day, he phoned me at home. I could hardly make out what he was saying. He wanted to invite me to a hockey game. He knew I liked hockey because after swimming, we'd stop at the snack bar for a coffee, and I'd chat with him about how the Leafs (Toronto Maple Leafs) were doing. He claimed to be a fan, but I suspect it was just something to talk about. Something easy. Something predictable. From what I gathered from the phone call, Bob had acquired some choice tickets for a world-cup game in Hamilton (about an hour away from where we were living), and he wanted me to join him. I wrongly assumed he needed me to get him there and that is why he was calling. I think I may have been noncommittal; you know, *I'll have to see* kind of thing, but eventually I agreed. I was thinking about getting him there in my car. It was winter. I'd have to bring his non-motorized chair. Could I get it in my smaller car? Where would I park? How clear were the sidewalks? What if the car broke down? And the washrooms! Oh, my goodness! I was apprehensive. When the day came, my reservations were compounded. It wasn't just Bob and I, but a few of his floor-residents as well. Bob had arranged a van for all of us. He may have tried to convey that on the phone, but I didn't get it. As you might expect, the group was a diverse one. One young woman was quite autistic. She was making continuous clucking noises with her mouth and repeating phrases from a television advertisement over and over again. I remember her being quite fearful of loud noises and there were many that night. Another was an armless small person (i.e., affected by dwarfism). He was a chain smoker. He had an able-bodied roommate who placed the cigarettes in his mouth. His companion seemed reasonably ambulatory, but he may have had a less noticeable disability. He was quiet, content to let his small friend do most of the talking while the two of them smoked. There was also a quadriplegic ex-biker (an accident victim). He came decked-out in his leathers! He was paralyzed from the neck down. He used a puffer to propel his motorized wheelchair. Bob's roommate Mike also came along. He was similarly conflicted with CP although his oral language was easier to understand than Bob's. There might have been a few more folks from Bob's floor, but I can't remember them all. And then of course, there was me. Just me. Yikes! I couldn't believe it. What did I get myself into?

The weather was horrible, and there was some discussion that the van driver would have to cancel. We went anyways. What was the worst thing that could happen, right? Well, there we were, all crammed into this wheelchair-accessible van in the dead of winter with nothing but the monotonous drone of the engine and the persistent creaking of the mechanisms used to restrain the wheelchairs in place to while-away the time. Then the van experienced a mechanical problem. The driver had to radio (no cell phones at that time) for a replacement van. We had to wait at the side of the road for about an hour before it showed up. Here's the part that is interesting. The van driver was worried. I was worried. However, the group I was with were not. I don't think they cared if they missed the hockey game. It was a night out and that's all that mattered. The fact that the replacement van came with a police escort to help us make the transfer was an added bonus, especially for the autistic lady who got great glee from the flashing police lights!

We finally got to the game. I didn't know how the ticket thing would work but somehow it did. Bob (or somebody) had made some prior arrangements. Ushers directed us through the throngs of people to a wheelchair-accessible section. Bob was right. They were great seats. I sat in a folding chair beside Bob and his roommate Mike. What I didn't know was that Bob and Mike had spiked a water bottle with booze and were getting progressively tipsy! Real tipsy. As I mentioned previously, Mike was a little more articulate than Bob. He told me in so many words that drunk CP isn't much different than regular CP. I had to laugh along with them. They were making fun of themselves just like regular buddies do. I was in their world now. It might not have been typical for me, but it was for them. They were having a great time. The game was an afterthought. The noise, the bustle of activity—it was a remarkable departure from the static routine of their daily existence. And, I was along for the ride, with no particular function other than to hang out with the group and enjoy the evening along with them.

I'll admit to being a bit conflicted during the event. This was not a group I would choose to hang out with. I will also admit to underestimating their ability to manage the evening, as complex as it was. They were on their own from the start to the finish. It didn't matter if I was there or not. And, for a brief moment in time, I was one of them, as much an artifact of their conduct and decision-making as they were. We were a group. If we had a good time or a lousy one, it was dependent on all of us, not just me. This is *reverse inclusion*. The evening, as it turned out, was a good one, and I found myself having a good time. I managed to poke through the veneer of my assumed role and relax, take in the evening and enjoy the impact it was having on them (and me).

Both these examples are of my assumption of *vanquishment*—the prevailing thought that a person's disability is a barrier that can't (perhaps even shouldn't) be crossed. If I hadn't been challenged by their push for normalization, Rita and Bob's group of friends would remain, in my eyes at least, restricted. They were of course, but they conquered their restrictions in such a matter-of-fact way, and in doing so, wrestled my faulty assumptions to the fore.

Over the years I have seen folks seamlessly integrate into the culture of disability. It's remarkable to watch them penetrate the *normal/abnormal* barrier. For them, it doesn't seem to be a sophisticated maneuver at all. It just seems natural. Their voice doesn't change when they interact as an adult might do to a small child. They use simple language but not *dumbed down*. Just clear and concise communication. If something is misunderstood, they say it. *You're going to have to try that again, I didn't get it,* said plainly and without judgement. They don't pretend they understand or let the meaning slip away. They stick with it. It's peer-to-peer talk and it's wonderful to see. I try to emulate this approach when I can. Films like *My Left Foot*, the story of Christy Brown the mouth-painter with CP, depict this element of *normalcy* in very touching ways. *King Gimp* is another one. In these films there are lots of examples of the natural flow of human interaction. It's not contrived, the stratification of roles gets washed out. It's as it should be. The irony I suppose, is the content of either of these films wouldn't be film-worthy if it wasn't for the unusual ways these two painters adapt to their craft as well as to the everyday tasks they encounter. It would be too *normal* to be interesting. I think that's the key, making their disability more of a filter for how their life is experienced rather than a barrier that prevents them from encountering full access.

I have been watching the Para-Olympics recently. Like others, I am struck by the competitive spirit among the athletes as they participate in their various events. But there is something else that intrigues me.

The presentation of each athletes' disability is all over the place. Some have one arm, some have no arms. Others have appendages that function as arms but are clearly not. The same can be said for legs. Some athletes are perceptually handicapped (i.e., vision or hearing). Some were once able-bodied and due to an accident or a debilitating disease, became disabled. Still others, probably most, were born with their impairments. The part that interests me is the event organizer's obsession with leveling the competitive playing-field through a classification system so competitors can compete within an equally disadvantaged group (more or less). No one can fault them for trying to make each competition fair for the athletes but here is my point, in doing so they may have wandered off the path of inclusivity. In my view the organizers' steadfast adherence to grouping the athletes according to their assumed disadvantage, may have inadvertently bent the structure of each event to resemble something the able-bodied public expect to see—a competition with winners and losers. For example, a one-legged swimmer might be placed in the same category as a two-legged swimmer but who is disadvantaged differently, having only one working arm. How one discerns the disadvantage of a missing arm vs. a missing leg in swimming is beyond me. Is the one who finishes ahead of the other truly the better swimmer? There is another thing involving the classification system that I noticed. Some athletes compete in the same race but are evaluated differently due to their classification. I saw a female para-swimmer break a world record in

in a heat even though she placed 4th, whereas the 1st-place finisher merely won the heat with no world record. The distinction was their classifications were different. So did we have the 4th-place finisher receive more adulation for her accomplishment of the world record than the 1st-place finisher? Or did the new world record holder discount her world record accomplishment because she did not win? It seemed an odd thing to reconcile for the athletes.

When I think about the arbitrary nature of the criteria used in the classification system, I wonder what this is doing for the spirit of inclusivity for these athletes. Is it a kind of imposed *vanquishment* exercise—the assumption of diminished performance? How do these athletes process these decisions? The Tristin Chernove case brought this to mind. He is a para-cyclist who recently withdrew from the Tokyo Para Olympic Games. Chernove incurred a spinal cord injury through an automobile accident in 2001. While adapting to his injury he became involved in para-cycling. His injury left him with a debilitating neuropathy affecting both the power and symmetry of his pedal stroke. Early in his para-cycling career he classified as a C2 competitor, and he competed quite successfully within that classification, gaining a podium finish in more than a few occasions. However, in his preparation for the 2020 Tokyo Para Olympic Games he was unexpectedly reclassified from C2 to C1. It was determined that his neuropathy had advanced (it was a degenerative condition) and impaired him further than it had in prior competitions. Chernove was disappointed with the organizer's decision and withdrew from the competition. Here's the thing. Chernove withdrew, not because he couldn't win, but rather, because he couldn't lose! He knew he was just marginally removed from the C2 designation and would likely dominate the C1 competition, something he found counter to the spirit of the Games. In an interview with CBC's Matt Galloway on *The Current*, he confessed to feeling awkward about the situation. He didn't want to deprive other athletes, ones more disadvantaged than he, an opportunity to stand on the biggest stage in the world. Shouldn't the level of disadvantage he would incur at C2, the more difficult classification, been his to make much as prize-fighters often do when the choose to fight above their weight class?

The subordination of levels of performance in this system seems to be a *stick in the spokes* of the wheel of inclusivity. The tug-of-war between the mutually exclusive goals of participation and the winning/

losing framework engendered in the Olympics is being tampered with. However, I think the para-athletes get it. They seem to be able to walk the line between both without losing sight of their real purpose. Their post-event interviews appear to acknowledge this and whether they stand on the podium or not is almost secondary to their participation at this elite level. They graciously accept their medals of course but, always express gratitude for just being there, participating in the greatest event in the world. I am less sure able-bodied spectators see the distinction as they do. Don't get me wrong. I think the advancement of para-competition is a wonderful thing for promoting inclusivity, but I think the type of hair-splitting that Chernove experienced may be taking the event slightly off course.

I often think Rita when she asked that benign question about participating in the school field day. She was born too soon. Her assets could have taken her places in competitive sports. Maybe they did. I never had much of an opportunity to follow her much past 5th grade. However, if she did, I'm certain it would have opened enormous opportunities for her. But beyond each athlete's participation is another consideration. Para-athletics provides a window for the able-bodied world to view para-culture as a celebration of adaptation, blunting further the distinction between themselves and those with severe impairments. I recognize, it's not quite the same as strapping LeBron James into a wheelchair and having him compete in wheelchair basketball or, having Michael Phelps swim with one arm bolted to his side. Para-athletics is not *reverse inclusion* but it's the next best thing. Yes, the performances are astonishing, but we always seem to have to add the qualifier, *given the extent of each athlete's disability,* inadvertently diluting the accomplishment. In these events we see withered limbs and vestiges of legs equipped with prosthetics of one form or another. We see them crash about, falling violently to the floor. They get up, shake it off and move on. They are not pieces of glass. We may cringe but they don't. They are warriors. We also see them hug and congratulate each other, celebrating their shared humanity, with full knowledge their own particular struggle is not unique to them. They know full well their accomplishment does not separate them from those who finish behind them. I think when we see this, we are transformed. We see an otherwise-abled person with their disability shoved well into the background. This can't be a bad thing.

Chapter 13: Where Are They Now?

I often wonder about the purpose I served—if, and perhaps how, the lives of my former students were impacted by what I attempted to do for them. Were they able to adapt, able to eke out enough success to experience a fuller sense of belonging than the sum of their circumstances might have predicted? Readers have gleaned from this memoir that many (but certainly not all) of these students had enormous challenges that quite possibly resulted in a life of disappointment, misadventure, and even anguish. I have bumped into a few of my former students now and again as adults. I've seen them in stores while shopping. I've seen them on the street. Some are alone. Some are with their partners. Some are with their children. Such incidents usually begin with uncomfortable eye-contact as the memories fall into place. Some recognize me and we chat cordially for a moment, but these moments are rare. Often there is just a nod of acknowledgement, and we go our separate ways. Of these, the outward signs point to layers of sadness, each piled on top of the other—the clothes they are wearing, or the beat-up car they are driving, or simply their demeanour. Their eyes, cold and empty, their mouth flat with despair. These tell the more complete story. Not always of course, but enough to make me wonder about the effort in the work, and its meaning.

I'll mention one student in particular, not because he was exceptional but because he illustrates how I think many of these uniquely challenged young people end up. Paul was in a high school program I headed up. The program was the same one Rosario, the Iditarod enthusiast was in. Readers will recall the program was for wayward students and my mission was to keep them in school as best as I could. When I had Paul in my class, he was a pimply-faced kid, angry at the world for dealing him a bad hand. He was smart enough but very dyslexic. His folks had split and there was lingering acrimony about the divorce. His parents shared custody of him, however, Paul often returned from weekends with his dad, rife with hostility. I assumed it had not gone well. Paul rebelled at just about everything—school rules, expectations for behaviour, others' aspirations for him. Yet, there was something in him that was endearing, something worth salvaging you might say. It would surface now and again. It might be a joke he shared with you, some goofy thing he did—something exposing a connection he was making with something or someone. I can remember enjoying that about him. One example stands out for me some thirty years later. I had an arrangement to take him and a classmate (also in the program) fishing once they accomplished certain goals. Upon earning his reward, he approached me with the most unusual request. He wondered if we could bring Kirk along. I was shocked. Kirk was well known in our school. He was a big lumbering kid with Down syndrome who in many ways behaved like a three-year-old, not the type teenagers choose to hang with, especially ones like Paul. For Paul to want to include Kirk in this activity was astonishing. Risky, socially, I would think. Not to get too sidetracked, the four of us went fishing on a pleasant Saturday afternoon. I enjoyed watching the lazy flow of juvenile impulses as the three of them engaged with one another, skipping stones and snooping under rocks for critters while waiting for fish to tug on their bobbers. It was wonderful. Paul had this in him, but he kept this part of himself well concealed.

Unfortunately, Paul squandered his time in my program, eventually drifting away. He became a "dropout". About three or four years after leaving, he walked in my classroom door out of the blue. He was a bit taller and had filled out with a noticeable paunch and a few straggly whiskers. His acne had cleared up, but he didn't look like he was taking care of himself. He had grungy clothes and shaggy, matted hair. We made small talk for a while. He reported having had a few jobs but confessed he'd been "canned" a few times, claiming his employers were unreasonable. It was typical Paul. The conversation veered a bit toward seriousness. He began castigating my program, the one that was supposed to turn his life around, claiming it a "f...g failure. Didn't do a damn thing for me!", I remember him saying. I think he was surprised when I agreed with him. Why he felt it necessary to tell me this was more of a mystery. I can only surmise that he had begun to realize his life, such as it was, was not unfolding as he, and perhaps others, thought it should. He was, of course, deflecting the blame as he was wont to do.

As I was working on this memoir, I did a search and found Paul had a Facebook page. I estimated he would be about 48 or 49. His profile listed him as an artist. I was curious about this, as I recall he was naturally good at sketching. I remember trying to encourage this talent. He liked ghoulish images. He would produce these wonderful life-sized caricatures, complete with decaying arms and faces, and with flabby flesh draping off exposed bones—all wonderful stuff if you are a teenage boy, I suppose.

I snooped through his Facebook page a bit more, feeling a bit like a voyeur. I was hoping to uncover paintings he had completed, maybe a reference to a showing in an art gallery—something that might confirm his success as an artist. There was nothing. Just a single tattoo he had done for a friend. I am not an expert on tattoo art, but it looked good enough to warrant a fee. His post accompanying the image suggested a sincere pride in the "tat". However, only two of his 346 "friends" seemed impressed enough to offer a comment. Still, people make a living at this type of thing, so who am I to judge. Maybe he had made an economic success of his life through this kind of art, but my fear is that he did not. If anything, I strongly suspect he just scraped through. Another post spoke of the importance of friendship and loyalty, all gushy stuff—the kind of thing I would have promoted back when he was in my program. This post was accompanied by a picture of him with a few friends who had taken him in. A period of couch surfing perhaps? Was he homeless? Another post, a few months later, claimed he was in a relationship. There was only one comment on that one.

"Congratulenz," it said. I found it curious that it was the only one. A brief scroll down revealed a sad message about a son he hadn't seen in years. "You're probably about 18 now," it said. "I just want you to know your dad loves you." *A two-line Facebook post…that's love?* I thought. The day fishing with Kirk seeped back into my memory as I read it. I was saddened by his inability to recognize the futility of this lament to his estranged child. I thought of his son reading it on the off-chance—his message in a cyber-bottle hoping to be discovered. The emptiness of it all was disheartening.

Constructing a biography from the fragments of a Facebook page is patently unfair. The heavy reliance on rickety inferences, mired in inexcusable bias, render it so. But I suspect the effigy of a life lived on the margins of society similar to Paul's, would be common amongst my former students. Not all, but many. I would estimate that about half the children I had over the years emerged at the other side of their schooling on the positive side of the ledger: holding down a job, able to maintain relationships, staying out of jail. I'll offer these examples. I attended a wedding of one of my students. She had graduated from college and became a teacher! I am certain that my influence on her success was shared with other notables, but I was proud to attend her wedding nonetheless. On another occasion, my car broke down and I limped into a small garage. The mechanic was a former student I had once busted for bringing some marijuana to school. I had him in one of my programs about ten years prior. He recognized me sitting in the waiting room and came out to tell me he was doing okay, holding down a job and was married with a couple of kids. The fact he wanted me to know this was telling. Not the Nobel Prize but good stuff. Once I received an email out of the blue from a student I had about 20 years prior. It came from a curious address, a Canadian Forces base. He wanted to say hello. He had tracked me down somehow, and he wanted to tell me he was enjoying a life in the military. He expressed gratitude for me helping him. I could not remember any specific contribution to his life I may have made, but I did remember him going through a very turbulent time with his folks. Just being there for him might have been what he was recognizing as important. Who knows?

How one defines a life well-lived is of course folly, and I cannot lay claim to knowing the ideal components of a successful life. Yes, there are the obvious ingredients—economic independence, social integration, a sense of well-being, and personal fulfillment. *Self-actualized* is a trendy term in psychology that seems to express the ideal for a life well-lived. Regardless, the components are undeniably subjective and the weight of each varies considerably over a life span. The optics are not always helpful in discerning one from the other, either. For example, a homeless person (rough campers they are often called) might express levels of fulfillment far and above those of a CEO of a national corporation—the former's freedom from responsibility may be at times be enviable to the latter who feels burdened by the crushing weight of the expectations imposed on them. However, this does not prevent us from making judgements. The point here is, if one takes stock of their own life and can check off a majority of the boxes, it is likely due to a healthy mixture of personal investment, help from others, and a large dollop of timely good fortune. The tiny nudge given to a snowball at the top of a hill blanketed with fresh snow does not account for the size of it at the bottom, but it wouldn't have grown without it. Of course, if it hits a rock and breaks apart on the way down, or if it rolls across a bare patch, its ultimate size will be diminished. However, once in motion, the route it takes is largely out of one's hands. But again, nothing would have happened without that tiny nudge. Is the provenance of the nudge the one that made the difference? Well, I'll leave that for others to decide, but I'll let the feeling that I was there at the top of that snowy hill, linger a bit longer.

Epilogue

At the beginning of this memoir, I cautioned readers that I would be guilty of isolating the cases I felt to be unusual, a departure from the expected. In doing so, I skipped over the many students I encountered who didn't stand out, the ones who didn't have anything particularly troubling that would classify them as uniquely interesting to readers. The ones with "humdrum" learning problems you might say. These would be the majority, and I would be remiss if I didn't mention them, as they surely sustained my interest in my chosen field over the four decades of my career. I'll mention them here, chancing that my brevity might unintentionally give them short shrift.

Children come into Special Education because they are deemed "behind" academically, socially, emotionally, or physically. The criteria can be a bit formulaic. For example, to determine if a child has a learning disability (LD), an academic discrepancy formula is invoked. Among the accumulation of evidence that supports this diagnosis are valid standardized measures of both academic proficiency and intelligence. The results must show that the academic performance is at least 1.5 standard deviations lower than the intellectual one. Mind-numbing, isn't it? In reality, such children's departure from "typical" defies that kind of precision. The important recognition is that they are behind their peers, but we must remember that a child's experience of being "atypical" can be as debilitating as any cognitively-based difficulty they might be encountering. I've mentioned the 3-Vs as a problem here as well. So, *catching-them-up* to where they should be is the principal occupation of the Special Educator, and this, I am pleased to say, was amongst my most rewarding tasks. I will add that *catching-them-up* was appropriate for most of my students but certainly not all, such as the unique individuals that inspired this memoir. The work in accomplishing this remediation, however, is pretty mundane and doesn't lend itself to compelling narrative. One isolates the skill deficits, arranges for tasks that might ameliorate these deficits, and then goes about the business of leading the child through them while providing as much systematic feedback as is appropriate. The simplicity of this statement belies the complexity of the process, but basically, that is the chore of the Special Educator, day in and day out. It's called compensatory education. It sounds bland, but if the discipline is executed with forethought and precision, it can be immensely interesting. So, I taught many children to read, spell, and learn mathematics that previously couldn't at a level that was commensurate with their age. In most cases, this achievement was significant enough for them to no longer require Special Education. When this happened, it was delightful to experience. Without this kind of success happening on a regular basis, I am certain I would not have been able to continue in my career.

It also must be said that I had fun along the way. I was able to do some things with these students that I would not have been able to do had I been a General Educator. I took them camping, hiking, and skiing. We built things: Adirondack chairs, modular picnic tables, and convertible step stool chairs for kitchens. There was no lack of motivation while they were working on these tasks. We sold them to raise money for things we wanted to do. The kids operated it like a business, keeping records of costs and figuring out their labour to arrive at the selling price. We built bird houses and then accompanied conservation officers in boats to place them along various watercourses. We conducted tons of fun experiments for science. For example, we built rockets from two-litre plastic pop bottles, energized by compressed air. By studying the relationship between the launch angle and lateral distance, they learned a practical use for geometry. It was rocket science! I had them make small cars powered by the springs in mouse traps. The students had drag races with them! I supplied them with match-box code kits and then hid a well-concealed five-dollar bill in the classroom. I'd give them a coded clue every day for them to decipher using their decoding kit. Only through the accumulation of clues could the prize be found. It kept them engaged for weeks on end, applying the full extent of their personal resources to the task. These kinds of things and much more! Having fun while learning was very important, but watching the children participate in activities with full engagement, driven by their interest in the task rather than my arbitrary insistence, was the most fun of all. But fun was a by-product, not the goal. The goal was to infuse academic learning into compelling activities. I mention all this for fear my previous accounts may lead one to think my work was consistently mired in strife. This would not be true.

Nearing the end, as I wrestle with the wording in these final few paragraphs, I feel compelled to address my motives in constructing these pages. True, it has been my *Covid Project*—the pandemic providing me with the time. But there was something else that was bubbling beneath the surface—something I have been wanting to say, and fear that if left unsaid, the people I know and care about might not understand. The work I did, indeed the work of many other Special Educators, is uniquely skilled and worthy of much more than polite gestures of appreciation for one's patience. My claim is that the work, when done well, is a blend of practices informed by knowledge, both psychological and pedagogical, orchestrated in the shadows, beyond the view of the less informed. By revealing these cases, I am hoping that I have triggered some discomfort in those readers who may have felt a sense of *knowing* that they were not entitled to.

Some of the courses I taught at the University of Wisconsin – Eau Claire were introductory courses for would-be Special Educators. In these courses, I would often site the latest research on retention. It seems Special Educators abandon their chosen field far too early. In this research, many would attest to being "burned out". To my would-be educators, I would pose the question, *Why is this so?* Invariably, the research pointed to teachers not feeling they were making enough headway. In psychological terms, *feeling like one is making headway* is referred to as *self-efficacy*. As I began to pen this final chapter, I received a notification on one of my newsfeeds that Albert Bandura passed away at the age of 95. Bandura was considered by many to be an intellectual giant in psychology. His work on influencing human behavior (i.e., intrinsic motivation) and the role of *self-efficacy* was foundational to my doctoral thesis, and many of the viewpoints I have isolated in this memoir were spawned from his seminal research. I found the news, although sad, to be a rather enchanting coincidence. I include a reference to him here as I feel it germane to all those teachers who act with intention. I have refrained from inserting a quote that encapsulates a snippet of Bandura's wisdom, as I fear explaining the context would steer the ship too far off course. I will attempt to paraphrase. Bandura was a theorist who was interested in human agency, the motives that fuel adaptive responses to what he calls "bewildering situational variation"[11]. Feeling you can act, *self-efficacy*, is essential, even if the circumstances appear irrevocably dire. This is the perspective the Special Educator must have. They must feel empowered—rightly able to fortify themselves with the tools of the craft knowing the path forward is a lonely one.

End Notes

[1] Rosenthal, R., Jacobson, L. (1968) Pygmalion in the classroom. *Urban Review 3*, 16-20. https://doi.org/10.1007/BF02322211

[2] Siegfried Engelmann was a professor of education at the University of Oregon beginning in 1970. He was the principal author of Direct Instruction, a uniquely designed approach to teaching core subjects combining scripted formats with highly incremental curricula. Among his more evocative publication titles are, *War against the schools' academic child abuse* (1992) and *Give your child a superior mind: a program for the preschool child* (1981) and *Preventing failure in the primary grades¹* (1997).

[3] Lindsley, O. R. (1990b). Precision teaching: By teachers for children. *Teaching Exceptional Children, 22(3)*, 10-15.

[4] Direct Instruction (DI) is a curricular approach designed by Siegfried Englemann (and others) in the 1970's. Initially it was for language acquisition (DISTAR). Eventually, reading and mathematic were added. Later, adjunct programs that taught spelling (Morphographic Spelling), Reading Comprehension, Corrective Reading and Critical Thinking were added to the DI inventory.

[5] Redl, F. and Wineman, D. (1952). *Controls from Within: Techniques for the Treatment of the Aggressive Child*. Glencoe, Ill.: The Free Press.

[6] Redl, F. and Wineman, D. (1951). *Children Who Hate*. Glencoe, Ill.: The Free Press

[7] Long, N. and Fecser, F. (1991). *Life Space Crisis Intervention* (https://www.lsci.org/about-us/our-mission-history/)

[8] Ozonoff, Beth L., Goodlin-Jones & Marjorie Solomon (2010). Evidence-based Assessments of Autism Spectrum Disorders in Children and Adolescents. *Journal of Clinical Child & Adolescent Psychology, 34*(3), 523-540.

[9] "Bruno Bettelheim, Autism and the Rhetoric of Scientific Authority". In *Autism and Representation*, (2007), Osteen, M. (Ed.). In 1967 Bruno Bettelheim published The Empty Fortress: *Infantile Autism and the Birth of the Self*, forever affecting the world's view of autism. Hailed by the popular press, the book showed how Bettelheim effectively treated three children with severe autism at the University

---

1.   https://archive.org/details/preventingfailur0000enge

of Chicago's Orthogenic School by applying psychoanalytic theory and milieu therapy. Children who had once exhibited bizarre antisocial behaviour were, in some cases, completely cured. No one had ever achieved such success with this enigmatic disorder. Although Bettelheim's book did have its critics, the overflow of praise from Bettelheim's advocates drowned out the voices of the few detractors. As a result, Bettelheim's thesis, that the infant's relationship with her "refrigerator mother" caused autism, soon became the accepted explanation in popular and in some professional circles. This notion has since been completely debunked but the deleterious effect it had on worried, guilt-ridden mothers, lingered long after the burning embers of Bettelheim's accusations were extinguished.

[10] Applied Behavioural Analysis (ABA): An evidence-based approach to studying behaviour as a function of reinforcement, both intentional reinforcement and unintentional reinforcement. The approach asks, 'What is sustaining the behaviour in the child's ecosystem?' It builds on a data-based approach to decision making.

[11] Bandura, Albert. (2006). *Toward a Psychology of Human Agency*. In Perspectives on Psychological Science, 2(2), pp. 164-171.

Also by Joseph Morin

Trekking On A Human Landscape
Villains, Victims & the Vanquished: A Memoir

About the Author

Joseph (Joe) Morin is a retired educator, having taught at every level in community school settings; elementary, middle, and secondary. Although most of his career was spent in Special Education, 5 of his 29 years of his K-12 experience was in the general education stream (Grades, 4, 5, 7, & 8). In addition to community school settings, he also taught at an outdoor school, a residential treatment center, and a provincial demonstration school. Upon retiring from K-12, he accepted a position at the University of Wisconsin – Eau Claire in the Department of Special Education where he taught pre-service teachers for 14 years.

In 1970 he received his initial certification from Toronto Teacher's College (closed in 1978). He proceeded with his degree requirements concurrently after accepting his first teaching assignment in Mississauga, Ontario in 1970. He eventually graduated from York University in Toronto as an undergraduate (B.A. Sociology, 1974), and the University of Toronto for his graduate degrees (M. Ed., 1976 and Ed.D., 1998). In addition to his academic qualifications, he holds certifications in elementary, middle, and secondary as well as a Specialist Certificate in Special Education.

He currently resides in Calgary Alberta Canada with his wife of 54 years. He has one daughter, and two grandchildren.

He can be reached for comment at morinje@icloud.com.